CW00408972

Zionward!

Help on the Way to the Better Land

By George Everard

Originally published in 1873.

It is a Christian's privilege to be now, by virtue of his union with Christ, a citizen of no mean city, even the heavenly Jerusalem. In his Surety and Representative, he has taken his seat in the heavenly places. He has "come unto Mount Zion, and unto the city of the living God, the heavenly Jerusalem, and to an innumerable company of angels, to the general assembly and Church of the first-born, which are written in Heaven, and to God the Judge of all, and to the spirits of just men made perfect, and to Jesus the Mediator of the new covenant, and to the blood of sprinkling, that speaks better things than that of Abel!"

It is well to realize the present position of honor, dignity and security, which belongs to all who have fled for refuge to Jesus, and have trusted in His atoning sacrifice. Such a one is no longer an exile, a stranger, a foreigner. He is a pardoned and accepted child, a fellow citizen with the saints, and of the household of God.

Nevertheless, a Christian has to journey for a while through a world abounding in evil. Peril is on every side. It is like the wilderness to Israel on their way to Canaan. There is oftentimes the dry and barren land, and wells of water are but few; foes are hovering near, and the way is difficult to find — so that a Christian needs help along the way.

It is this which I desire to give in the following pages. They have been written at various times during the last few years, but have all had somewhat of the same object — to guide and strengthen and comfort believers on their pilgrimage to Zion.

They tell of the ladder of mercy which our Father has set up, as the one way of access to Himself.

They tell of that word of truth, and those purposes of grace there revealed, which are as sure and steadfast as the Rock which stands immovable through a thousand storms.

They tell of that Fountain of atoning blood to which pilgrims must resort for daily cleansing.

They tell of that Door into the presence-chamber of Jehovah, which stands open for all who will enter thereby. We need evermore the spirit of prayer, the eye looking upward for grace and help.

Nor must the hand be idle, for we must be workers in our Lord's vineyard.

And, however weak the Christian may be in himself — yet there is strength for the strengthless in all times, of toil, dreariness, or suffering.

And we learn too that the Christian life should progress. The well of grace within the soul must evermore be deepened; and we must strive after a closer walk, and a nearer fellowship with God. The faithful, eternal God, shall be the believer's unchanging support. His everlasting arms shall uphold you even in the dark valley and in the swellings of Jordan, and shall convey you safely to the City of habitation — the Home of God's beloved ones.

May the Spirit of God make use of these pages to comfort and edify some of the weak and tried ones of the flock of Christ!

The Heavenly Ladder — and How to Climb it

Frequently does God give to His people their sweetest comforts in their saddest hours. Look at Jacob as he left Beersheba and went on his way toward Haran. When wearied with his journey he lay down to sleep, the cold sod was his couch — a stone his pillow — the sky above his curtain. Sorrowful indeed that night must have been the heart of the patriarch. He had just parted from the father and mother whom he dearly loved. He had just left behind him the home of his childhood. He was setting out on a long and dangerous journey, with no companion but the staff he carried in his hand. Yet how gracious is God! "Like as a father pities his children, so the Lord pities those who fear Him."

This — the darkest, the most cheerless night in Jacob's life, became the brightest. Never before had he been so bereft of human comfort. Never before had God so graciously revealed Himself to His servant. He saw a vision of a ladder reaching from earth to Heaven. Upon it he saw the angels ascending and descending. Above it, stood the Lord God, who spoke to him words of blessed encouragement. He had thought he was alone; but he was not, for angels were there to minister to him. He had thought his journey was about to be a solitary one; but the Lord promised that He Himself would accompany him, and preserve him from the dangers of the way. And God promised him still more — that land upon which he was lying as a stranger should be given to him and to his seed. He who was now a lonely pilgrim — would become a great people, and through him should come the long-promised Messiah — that seed of Abraham in whom all families of the earth should be blessed.

Here is the account: "Jacob left Beersheba and set out for Haran. When he reached a certain place, he stopped for the night because the sun had set. Taking one of the stones there, he put it under his head and lay down to sleep. He had a dream in which he saw a ladder resting on the earth, with its top reaching to heaven, and the angels of God were ascending and descending on it. There above it stood the LORD, and he said: I am the LORD, the God of your father Abraham and the God of Isaac. I will give you and your descendants the land on which you are lying. Your descendants will be like the dust of the earth, and you will spread out to the west and to the east, to the north and to the south. All peoples on earth will be blessed through you and your offspring. I am with you and will watch over you wherever you go, and I will bring you back to this land. I will not leave you until I have done what I have promised you." Genesis 28:10-15

I shall now leave the history of the patriarch, and consider only the ladder which he saw in his vision. Christ often used similitudes — and so may we. Let that ladder teach us precious lessons as to the way of life. It plainly points to Christ and His salvation. It tells us of Him who is the only Mediator between God and man. It tells us how, lost and fallen though we are, we may yet climb the skies, and enter "that city which has foundations, whose Builder and Maker is God." Let me first give you a few thoughts with respect to the ladder itself, and then consider how we may climb it.

I. A few thoughts with respect to the ladder itself.

1. This ladder is the only communication between earth and heaven — between a holy God and sinful men. Sin has made a vast chasm — a vast separation between the

creature and the Creator. "Your iniquities have separated between you and your God." (Isaiah 59:2.) There is a two-fold reason for this. On the one hand, our sins have brought against us the sword of Divine justice: the degree has gone forth from the council-chamber of Heaven, "The wages of sin is death!" "The soul that sins it shall die!"

On the other hand, our guilty hearts shrink from the presence of our righteous Judge. We fear to approach One whom our sins have so grievously offended. The accusing conscience cries out with Simon Peter, "Depart from me, for I am a sinful man, O Lord."

Here is the separation — how can it be overcome? How can the breach be made up? How can God and man again walk together as friends? No efforts of our own — no self-made ladders can ever affect it. Our doings — our prayers — our repentance — cannot bring us near to God. They cannot atone for past guilt; they cannot remove the penalty of a broken law; they cannot pacify a fearful conscience. The best we can do is in itself sinful and polluted, and therefore needs forgiveness before it can be accepted; still less then can it be to us any ground of hope. Now God knows this: He has said, "O Israel, you have destroyed yourself, but in Me is your help."

So in His great mercy He has provided a means whereby we may return to Him. With His own hand He has let down a ladder of grace from above. He has given Jesus to be our Savior — to live and die for us. "God so loved the world that He gave His only-begotten Son, that whoever believes in Him should not perish, but have everlasting life." (John 3:16.) "Herein is love, not that we loved God, but that He loved us, and sent His Son to be the atoning sacrifice for our sins." (1 John 4:10.)

Never be it forgotten that this is the only way by which the sinner can return to God. Nothing else can possibly avail: "There is no other name under Heaven given among men whereby we must be saved." (Acts 4:12.) Has not Jesus said Himself, "I am the way — no man comes unto the Father but by Me?"

2. This ladder is firmly fixed and perfectly safe. Before climbing a ladder, you need to know whether it will bear you — and whether you can safely trust yourself to it. This ladder of which I speak is so firm, so safe — you never need fear for a single moment to venture your weight upon it. It has been fixed by God's own hand. Whatever man does often falls to the ground, often fails of its purpose — whatever God does stands fast forever: "He works all things after the counsel of His own will." (Ephesians 1:11.)

The erecting of this ladder is the fulfillment of the everlasting purpose of the Most High. Before ever man had fallen — before ever the world was made, was the plan of salvation determined upon. Then, in the fullness of time, Jesus came to carry out this plan — to seek and to save those who were lost. Safely, then, may we trust ourselves to this ladder, for it is God's own appointed way by which sinners may be saved.

Again, you may be sure it is firm and safe, for none have ever been able to move it. How often have wicked men tried to throw it down! See all the persecutions which have raged against Christ's Church! See the myriads who have been led to the scaffold or the stake for their faithfulness to Christ's name! See how often the skeptic or the infidel has tried to prove the Bible to be false, and Christianity a lie — but it has ever been in vain. Still is the

religion of Jesus known and loved as the sinner's only
hope, and the mourner's only comfort.

And how Satan has tried to throw down this ladder!
When Christ was upon earth, did not Satan thrice tempt
Him in the wilderness? And when he could not tempt Him
to turn aside a single hair's breadth from the path of duty,
did he not compass His death? Did he not stir up the
covetousness of Judas and the malice of the chief priests?
Yet, what was his success? The cross which was the very
masterpiece of the devil's wickedness — became the chief
means of the overthrow of his kingdom of darkness!

The cross became the very ladder of salvation to the
sinner!

It became the resting-place of every heavy-laden
conscience.

There we see mercy and truth meet together —
righteousness and peace kiss each other.

There we see God glorified — yet the sinner saved;
the law honored — and yet man forgiven.

"God forbid that I should glory," says the great
Apostle, "save in the cross of our Lord Jesus Christ, by
which the world is crucified to me, and I unto the world."
(Galatians 6:14.)

Again, you may know that this ladder is firm and safe,
for it has been tried by believers ever since the world
began. All who have ever been saved, have been saved by
Christ: Abel, Enoch, Noah, Abraham, Isaac and Jacob —

prophets, apostles, martyrs — all the people of God in each age have reached Heaven by this ladder.

And who has ever found it to fail? Who has ever been able to say, "I went to Christ, but it was in vain — He could not, or He would not save me." Never one! Multitudes have refused to come to Him; multitudes have professed to come, who yet in heart turned away — but never one truly went to Jesus in humble faith, in earnest prayer, but found the word of promise true: "Him that comes unto Me, I will never cast out." (John 6.37.) With one voice they all declare that He has done for them far more than ever they could have expected.

Oh, anxious, trembling sinner — cast away your dark, distrustful thoughts; venture your soul on Christ! He is a tried Savior — He cannot, He will not disappoint you!

Come sinner, with your load of woe,
And to your gracious Savior go;
He turns no beggar from His door —
He saves and blesses evermore.

3. Every step, every rung of this ladder is some spiritual blessing.

All that the sinner needs from first to last is found in Christ, and in Him alone. From the first sigh of a broken heart, from the first longing after salvation, from the first breathing of prayer in the soul, to the first note of praise in glory — all grace must come from Christ. Do not imagine you are to come to Christ at the beginning of your Christian course, but that the rest of it you must accomplish by your own energy or perseverance. Far, far otherwise. Of yourself you can neither retain the grace you have, nor take one single step forward. "Without Christ you can do nothing" — but through Christ strengthening you, you may do all things. Mark the four rungs of this ladder, described by Paul: "It is because of Him that you are in Christ Jesus, who has become for us . . .

Wisdom,
Righteousness,
Sanctification, and
Redemption." 1 Corinthians 1:30

Are you very blind, knowing but little of yourself, little of your own heart, still less of God and the way to Zion? Jesus says, "I will be Your Wisdom: I will teach you out of My Word; I will open your understanding, that you may learn all things needful for your salvation."

Are you very sinful — very unworthy? Jesus says, "I will be your Righteousness: My Blood shall cleanse you from every spot of guilt; My Robe of Righteousness shall cover you, and make you perfect in the eye of God."

Do you feel depraved and corrupt within — very unfit for the fellowship of the saints around the throne? Jesus says, "I will be your Sanctification: I will put my Spirit within you, I will write my Law upon your heart, I will cleanse you from all your filthiness and from all your idols, I will renew you in my own image, I will make you fit for the inheritance of the saints in light."

Are you compassed about by manifold evils, painful infirmities, distressing doubts, trials, temptations, cares, and sorrows? Jesus says, "I will be your Redemption: I will deliver you from them all; in My own good time I will set you free; every fear shall prove a false prophet; from death itself will I redeem you at the day of My appearing!"

Yes, in Jesus is every need met. "Blessed be the God and Father of our Lord Jesus Christ, who has blessed us with all spiritual blessings in heavenly places, in Christ." (Ephesians 1:3.) "My God shall supply all your need according to His riches in glory, by Christ Jesus." (Philippians 1:19.) "It has pleased the Father that in Him should all fullness dwell." (Colossians 1:19.)

> When you look at yourself, you may indeed say —
> "What without You can I be?
> What without You can I do?"

> But when you look at Christ, you may add —
> "I lay my wants on Jesus —
> All fullness dwells in Him;
> He heals all my diseases,
> He does my soul redeem!"

4. This ladder reaches the very lowest spot on earth's surface. It reaches to the guiltiest, the most degraded sinner to be found on earth. It reaches not lower than this — not to Hell — for there is no ladder of salvation there, no gracious invitation, no promise of pardon, no voice of a merciful Savior heard there. But it does reach to the blackest sinner — the most hardened sinner to be found on this side the grave: "Jesus is able to save to the uttermost all who come to God by Him."

See that malefactor hanging by the side of Jesus — as near as he was to Hell, yet this ladder reached to him. He owned his guilt. He called upon Christ: "Lord, remember me, when You come into Your kingdom." And his prayer was heard — Jesus said to him, "Today shall you be with Me in Paradise."

See those wicked Corinthians — what were they once? "Sexually immoral, idolaters, adulterers, male prostitutes, homosexual offenders, thieves, greedy, drunkards, slanderers, swindlers" (1 Corinthians 6:9-10) — yet this ladder reached to them! They were "washed, sanctified, and justified in the name of the Lord Jesus, and by the Spirit of our God."

It is even so now — there is still mercy for the chief of sinners. Go to the lowest dens of iniquity — go to the worst haunts of vice — go to the cottage or the room where the voice of prayer has never been heard, where the Bible has never been read, where the walls could bear witness to scenes of vileness and profligacy of which it is a shame even to speak — go there, and find out the very vilest, and tell such an one, "There is mercy for you!" "There is a welcome in the heart of God for you!" "There is cleansing in the open fountain for you!" Only acknowledge your iniquity, only confess it and forsake it, and Jesus is ready to save you — even you. Though your heart is as hard as the nether millstone — yet He will soften it. Though your sins are for multitude as the sand upon the seashore, though they be for magnitude as the great mountains of the earth — yet all shall be forgiven." "Come now, and let us reason together, says the Lord: though your sins are as scarlet, they shall be as white as snow; though they are red like crimson, they shall be as wool." (Isaiah 1:18.) "The blood of Jesus Christ, God's Son, cleanses from all sin."

Oh, what comfort is here for the despairing sinner! There is no depth of misery or sin upon earth to which this ladder reaches not.

5. The uppermost step of this ladder reaches to the Father's house. If the lowest step reaches very low, the

highest reaches very high. We read in the vision of Jacob, "Behold a ladder set upon the earth — and the top of it reached unto Heaven." Oh, what a contrast between the lowest and highest steps of the ladder! The lowest step is here on earth, in the midst of sin, sorrow, temptation, disease, and death. The highest step reaches to that place where these things can never enter, where "God shall wipe away all tears from their eyes — and there shall be no more death, neither sorrow, nor crying, neither shall there be any more pain. For the former things have passed away." (Rev. 21.4.)

Then shall the rejoicing spirit bid an everlasting "Good-bye," to all that now weighs heavy upon his heart. Then shall he say, "Farewell all my sad and sorrowful hours! Farewell doubts and fears! Farewell cares and anxieties! Farewell crosses and disappointments! Farewell sickness, suffering, and death!"

Then shall he breathe the pure and peaceful atmosphere of the heavenly Canaan. Then shall he drink of those unspeakable joys which are at God's right hand. Then shall he be forever in the presence of the Lamb! "They shall hunger no more, neither thirst any more; neither shall the sun light on them, nor any heat. For the Lamb which is in the midst of the throne shall feed them, and shall lead them to living fountains of water." (Rev. 7.16, 17.)

Oh, how thankful should we then be for this heavenly ladder! Justly might we have been left to reap the bitter fruits of our sins — justly might we have been left in our lost and fallen state. But God has looked upon us in pity and compassion. "He has not dealt with us after our sins, nor rewarded us according to our iniquities." He has opened to us a door of mercy. He has devised means by which His banished ones may not be expelled from Him. He has given us this ladder — so firm, so safe, so all-sufficient — reaching down to us in our deepest wretchedness and woe — reaching upward to His own blessed abode. Oh, that our hearts might continually echo those words of Paul, "Thanks be to God for His unspeakable gift""

II. But now let us inquire how may we climb this heavenly ladder? How may we so tread it as safely to reach the Father's house?

1. Do not shrink from pain-taking effort — from real exertion. If you wished to reach some lofty eminence, it would not be enough for a ladder to be set up which would bring you to it. If you were to sit down at the foot of this ladder — if you were merely to look at it or speak of it, or wish you were at the top, what would it avail? All would be in vain, unless you put your foot upon it, unless you took the pains and trouble to climb it for yourselves.

So it is in the religion of Jesus Christ; it is all in vain to indulge in empty idle wishes. Sitting down at the foot of the ladder — hearing of Christ, speaking of Christ, thinking of Christ, wishing to be a Christian — will never save you. By the power of the Holy Spirit, you must come to Christ for yourself, you must seek Christ for yourself. Whatever efforts it may cost you, whatever pains or trouble it may require, relying on the help of the same Almighty Spirit — you must be willing to give it.

Say not because there is this ladder, because there is a Savior, that all is well. To many a one in a future state the saddest thought of all will be this, "There was a ladder — but I would not use it!

There was a Savior — but I would not go to Him!

There was mercy, but I would not seek it!

There was an open Heaven set before me, but I refused to enter in!"

Beware too of a religion that requires no pains, no trouble, no self-denial, no crucifying the flesh, no time to be specially set apart for it — a religion that leaves you much as it finds you. Such a religion may be enough to blind the conscience, but it is not the religion of the Bible — it is not the religion which Christ will own as the work of His Spirit in the heart. Listen to the words of our Divine Master: "The kingdom of Heaven suffers violence, and the violent take it by force!" (Matthew 11.12.) "Strive to enter in at the strait gate!" (Luke 13.24.) "Labor not for the food which perishes, but for that food which endures to everlasting life, which the Son of Man shall give unto you." (John 6.27.)

2. Place your foot upon the lowest step. Don't imagine you must raise yourself a few inches, or a few feet from the ground — before you step upon this ladder. Don't imagine you must make yourself a little better, or your sins a little less, or your heart a little more penitent — before you come to Christ: in this way you will never, never succeed. Rather come to Him just as you are — exactly as you are at this moment — and He will make you all you need to be. Come to Him as a thoroughly vile, good-for-nothing sinner! Tell Him you have not a single good thing which you can bring to recommend you to His favor. Tell Him you have nothing of your own but misery, need, and sin; but that you come depending upon His own free promise, and His all-atoning blood.

Jesus will receive you just as you are! Though your sins are many, though your heart is hard — yet will He receive you; and receiving you, will supply every possible need. Oh, go to Jesus with those words, so precious to many a troubled soul:

Just as I am — without one plea,
But that Your blood was shed for me,
And that you bid me come to Thee —
O Lamb of God, I come!

Just as I am — and waiting not
To rid my soul of one dark blot,
To You, whose blood can cleanse each spot —
O Lamb of God, I come!

Just as I am — poor, wretched, blind;
Sight, riches, healing of the mind,
Yes, all I need, in You to find —
O Lamb of God, I come!

III. Strive after continual progress. Do not be satisfied with low attainments. A man has not reached the top of a ladder when he has stepped upon the lowest round, but he ascends it step by step. So it is in the course of the Christian: "The path of the just is as the shining light, which shines more and more unto the perfect day." (Proverbs 4:16.)

We have a beautiful illustration of this in the life of Paul. Though so far above most all others, both in Christian experience and devotedness of life, still he was not content — he aimed at a yet higher standard. He writes, "Brothers, I do not consider myself yet to have taken hold of it. But one thing I do: Forgetting what is behind and straining toward what is ahead, I press on toward the goal to win the prize for which God has called me heavenward in Christ Jesus!" Philippians 3:13-14

Let it be your aim to follow in the Apostle's footsteps. Strive every day to get a step higher on the heavenly ladder. Strive to become more humble, more holy, more faithful, more useful, more prayerful — in short more Christ-like! "Make every effort to add to your faith goodness; and to goodness, knowledge; and to knowledge, self-control; and to self-control, perseverance; and to perseverance, godliness; and to godliness, brotherly kindness; and to brotherly kindness, love. For if you possess these qualities in increasing measure, they will keep you from being ineffective and unproductive in your knowledge of our Lord Jesus Christ!" 2 Peter 1:5-8

> Nearer my God, to Thee —
> Nearer to Thee!
> E'en though it be a cross
> That raises me;
> Still all my song shall be
> Nearer, my God, to Thee —
> Nearer to Thee!

4. Carry with you no needless burden. If a man were to attempt to climb a high ladder, carrying with him a heavy load, he would find it very difficult, if not impossible, to reach the top. So, if the Christian carries with him unnecessary burdens, it will greatly impede and hinder him. Oh, cast every weight aside! Leave it at the foot of the ladder. Whatever it is that proves a hindrance and a snare to you — by God's help cast it away.

We are told that when Jesus called Bartimeus, "He cast away his garment, and arose and came to Him." So, do you cast away that which keeps you back.

Is it the love of the world in any of its various shapes?

Is it the love of money?

Is it the love of pleasure?

Is it the desire for display?

Is it the concern to win the praise of man?

Remember it is written, "The world passes away, and the lust thereof: if any man loves the world, the love of the Father is not in him." (1 John 2:15-17.)

Is it some secret sin known only to God and yourself?

Is it some injurious habit, that often breaks your peace and wounds your soul?

Is it some cherished resentment?

Is it an angry or passionate temper that you will not curb?

Is it an oppressive weight of earthly care, which unfits you for communion with God and meditation upon His Word?

Oh, forsake that sin! Watch against that unruly temper! Cast that care "upon Him who cares for you. "Let us lay aside every weight, and the sin which so easily besets us, and let us run with patience the race that is set before us!" (Hebrews 12.1.)

5. Mind where you place your foot. In climbing a ladder, a man must be careful about his footing — a false step, and he may fall. It may be the breaking of a limb — it may be his death! So let the Christian be very watchful where his foot is found. Keep as far as possible out of the reach of danger. Let not your foot be found in scenes where the Tempter is accustomed to come. Mingle not in scenes of worldly gaiety or reveling. You carry with you a wicked and deceitful heart, so that a very small temptation may turn you aside. An hour spent in bad company has often been the prelude to a life of wretchedness and sin. A visit to a public-house, or a dancing-room, has often been the first step on the road to ruin.

On the other hand, let your foot be often treading the courts of the Lord's house. Let no grass grow on the path that leads you to the throne of grace. Frequent the society of those who will help you, and converse with you on spiritual subjects. I repeat it — be very careful as to your footing!

Remember that to the true believer many dark hours, much loss of inward peace, may follow a single false step, a single turning aside out of the narrow path. Very little while had Christian and Hopeful turned into By-path Meadow before they were in Doubting Castle. "Enter not into the path of the wicked, and go not in the way of evil men." "Avoid it, pass not by it, turn from it and pass away." "Ponder the path of your feet, and let all your ways be established. Turn not to the right hand nor to the left — remove your foot from evil." (Proverbs 4:14, 15:26, 27.)

6. Keep fast hold. It will not do to take hold of a ladder loosely, with one finger or with one hand — it needs a tight firm grasp with both hands to ensure safety. So do you by strong faith, take a firm grasp on Christ. Relying upon the help of His Spirit . . .

cling to Him with all your heart and with all your soul!

Cling to His great and precious promises!

Cling to His cross as all your hope and salvation!

Cling to Him as your ever-living, ever-loving, ever-faithful Friend and Savior!

Cling to Him in your days of joy!

Cling to Him in your days of sadness and sorrow!

Cling to Him in life and in death — never let Him go!

He says to you, "I will never leave you nor forsake you!" Return back to Him His own promise, and say, "Lord, by Your grace assisting me, I will never leave You nor forsake You!"

7. Lastly. Let your eye ever be upward. If a man looks down a ladder when he is climbing it, he may perhaps grow dizzy and fall. While he looks upward he is safe. So here again is a lesson for the Christian. You must not look downwards — you must not look back to this perishing world.

The description given of a faithful minister, in Bunyan's great allegory, may teach a lesson to every believer: He saw hanging up against the wall, a picture of a very serious person: "He had eyes lifted up to Heaven. The best of books in his hand. The law of truth was written upon his lips. The world was behind his back."

Oh, let it be so with you!

Keep the Word of God your constant companion.

This world, with all it has to offer — cast behind your back.

Let your eyes be lifted up to Heaven.

Keep your eyes fixed on Jesus.

See Him standing on your behalf at God's right hand, ready to help you in every time of need.

See Him waiting to receive your every petition and to give you fresh supplies of His quickening Spirit.

See Him holding in His hand for you, a crown of glory.

See Him waiting to greet you with a joyful welcome when your course is finished.

So shall you be kept from falling — so shall you leave behind you doubts and fears that once distressed you — so shall you taste more and more the fruits of that land of promise to which you are hastening — so shall the warm beams of the Sun of Righteousness shine more and more into your heart, and fill you with all joy and peace in believing.

Reader, I have spoken of this heavenly ladder — let me now plainly put it to your conscience:

Is your foot yet upon it?

Have you ever yet realized that through sin, you yourself are lost and perishing?

Do you feel that none but Jesus can save you?

Have you come to Him?

Have you taken hold of Him by heart-faith?

Have you entrusted your soul to His care, as an almighty and all-merciful Savior?

Do you love Him?

Do you serve Him?

Do you follow Him?

These are solemn questions: for, bear in mind, there is another ladder. It is true there is God's ladder — Christ and His salvation, which leads to Heaven — but there is the devil's ladder, which leads down to Hell.

Upon the former you may see here and there one and another, with much difficulty, with many discouragements, striving to ascend.

Upon the latter you may see multitudes — multitudes, going down quick into Hell. Step by step — lower and lower. Alas, there are very many hastening to the pit of everlasting destruction!

But what are the steps of this ladder? I will tell you. Open sins — such as lying, swearing, drinking, profligacy, and such like. Neglect of religion, an unread Bible, days spent without prayer, formal services, warnings unheeded, faithful sermons disregarded, hardness of heart, putting off repentance until a future day. Such are some of the steps on the downward ladder. You never know when the last step on either ladder may be taken! You do no know but that last step may be taken this very day. If your soul is safe — if you are indeed trusting in Jesus, before tomorrow's dawn your pilgrimage may be over — your crown may be won. But if not — if you still are unpardoned and unsaved — before another sun shall rise you may be a castaway — the door of hope may be shut — your soul may be eternally lost!

What then ought you to do? Without one moment's delay step off the one ladder and upon the other. Cast away every sin — every false hope; kneel at the feet of Jesus, confess to Him your past guilt, and commit your eternal interests into His hands.

"Believe on the Lord Jesus Christ, and you shall be saved." (Acts 16.31.)

"Behold, now is the accepted time; behold, now is the day of salvation." (2 Corinthians 11.2.)

Firm as a Rock!

A few miles from the southern shores of England, and not far from many a sunken rock, stands the Seamen's Friend. For more than a century, in spite of stormy wind and tempest, the Eddystone lighthouse has stood firm and unmovable, giving light and saving life, warning the mariner away from hidden perils, and guiding into the friendly harbor many a gallant ship that might otherwise have been wrecked.

Its construction is remarkable. A predecessor, built of less durable materials, had been swept away during a storm, and all within perished. Hence it was that special care was taken in securing its stability. Fourteen courses of huge blocks of granite and Portland stone, each from one to two tons, were dovetailed into the solid rock and into each other; then upon this building, almost as solid as the rock beneath it, was placed the lantern with its various lights, directing the sailor along his course, and pointing out the way to the port a few leagues distant.

The Word of God is somewhat like this lighthouse. The comparison has often been made, and it is a true one. The Word bears a light. It is a bright lamp for those that are voyaging over the dark and stormy waves of this troublesome world. It bids men away from those perilous rocks of error, of licentiousness, of love of gold or pleasure — on which too many souls founder and perish. It reveals Christ, the true Harbor of Refuge, and manifests to men how, amidst the roaring of the tempest — they may yet find their true and only rest in Him.

Especially would I ask the attention of the reader to the consideration of the stability of God's Word — it is the very thought we most need.

There are continually fresh changes and sorrows in many homes. Families once unbroken — mourn the loss of a parent, a child, a brother or sister. Those in affluence are brought low, and means fail them. Those beforetime strong and healthy — know the painfulness of disease and infirmity. Even those most desolate may find a relief from their heavy burden of sorrow and anxiety. God's mighty providence, His tender, fatherly compassions, His faithfulness, His own blessed revelation of Himself in His Word — these abide, and we doubt not at such seasons become to many a soul, a light more bright and cheering than ever before.

Wide as the world is Your command,
Vast as eternity Your love,
Firm as a rock Your truth shall stand
When rolling years shall cease to move.

Firm as a rock God's truth has stood, and shall stand forever. Let us go back to the illustration that has been employed. The lighthouse has stood firm amidst the storms of a century, because it is securely fixed upon the solid rock; in fact, it is one with it — each stone is so closely connected with the rest and with the rock beneath, that all the violence of the tempest has been in vain.

Even so God's Word, and every part of it, rests upon the rock of His truth. It is one Book, though written at various times and by different writers. Each part is connected with every other part, and the whole permeated by the teaching of the ever blessed Spirit. So that it cannot be destroyed; it cannot fall, whatever assaults may be made upon it. It is true, and that which is true shall abide as long as the God of truth Himself.

Old objections may appear in new forms — unfriendly criticism may suggest its doubts, theories in science may conflict with received interpretations. Yet be not afraid — forget not the confirmation God's Word has been receiving from the very beginning. Difficulties that seemed once almost insuperable, have been removed by the discovery of some historical monument of early times. Again and again has true science proved the handmaid of Scriptural revelation. The secret places of the earth have given up some witness to God's truth — and all tend to establish our confidence. They teach us that our old Bible is no cunningly-devised fable, but that it speaks truth and only truth.

The moral proofs of the inspiration of Holy Writ are likewise irrefutable. It suits men in every nation alike. It brings blessing and peace wherever it comes. By the grace of the Holy Spirit, it becomes the instrument of a new and better life to men who have been aforetime sunken in every kind of evil. It gives rest to wearied and burdened consciences, and calms the troubled and sorrowing spirit.

Therefore, amidst increasing unbelief on all sides, let us still be steadfast and hopeful. All flesh fades like the grass, and the glory of man like the withering flower; yes, the very rocks shall be moved out of their place, and Heaven and earth shall pass away, the elements shall melt with fervent heat, and things temporal shall give place to the things that are eternal — but know for a surety that the Word of our God shall stand forever.

Firm as a rock are those exceeding great and precious promises which the Word sets before us. The promises of earthly friends may greatly comfort us in times of deep necessity: the promise of their sympathy, of their readiness to assist us in bearing some heavy weight of anxiety, of their presence in some dark hour to which we look forward — these may cheer and help us, yet but a little way can such help go. We may be looking forward to a promised visit — but our expected friend may be compelled to travel many a mile in an opposite direction. We may anxiously be on the look-out for a special letter — but the hand that should write it may be lying cold and motionless. We may wait for a few pounds to meet a pressing debt — but heavy losses may have overtaken one who would otherwise gladly have kept his word to us.

Many a promise fails, because the promiser is unable to keep it. Many a one is left unfulfilled, because of human infirmity, forgetfulness, change of feeling, or the like. So that it is never wise to lean too much on the arm of flesh, or to expect too much even from the kindest or most faithful among men.

But with Divine promises it is otherwise:
they have a height and depth, a length and breadth that surpass our highest conceptions,
they reach the whole circumference of human necessity,
they extend through all time,
they anticipate all difficulties,
they satisfy all holy desires,
they open out a field for bright and glorious anticipations that would never otherwise have entered into the heart of man.

They meet us in our felt sinfulness — by the declaration of free and perfect forgiveness; yes more, by the bestowment of a righteousness in which the eye of God can discern no blemish.

They meet us in our consciousness of deadness and pollution and weakness — by the offered gift of the Comforter, the Holy Spirit, to renew the heart in holiness and in love, to quicken and strengthen every good desire, and to mortify all that is evil.

They meet us in our manifold distresses and perplexities — by holding out to us the assurance of Fatherly love and all-sufficient grace.

They meet us on the threshold of the grave — by reminding us of One who, in the furnace and in the flood alike, will not fail to stand by those who trust in Him.

They meet us in our anticipations of the great and glorious future — by pointing us upward to the mansions of the Father's house, and forward to the day of the Lord, when the King will take His people to live and reign with Him forever and ever.

Reader, place your foot firmly here! Rest your soul on the promises — they cannot fail you. "I may tremble on the Rock, but the Rock will not tremble under me," was the saying of an Irish lad when asked of his hope for the future. Tremble though you may as you remember your sins, or look out into the years yet to come, with all the sorrow and care they may bring you — yet look beyond all this. Hear the voice of Him that speaks to you of pardon for all your offences, and of upholding strength through your pilgrimage, and rejoice in Him.

Very precious is the prayer of David when he reminds God of His promise, relies upon it, and looks forward to its fulfillment: "Now, O Lord God, You are that God, and Your words are true, and You have promised this goodness unto Your servant. Therefore now let it please You to bless the house of Your servant; for You, O Lord God, have spoken it." Hence it is that, firm on the sure rock of God's promises, you may leave calmly the past, the present, and the future to Him who will never leave you nor forsake you. He will . . .

guard you in all danger,

support you in all tribulation, and

bring you by the right way to the haven of everlasting rest.

It was thus that Asaph reposed in God after the struggle with unbelief, recorded in the seventy-third Psalm. (See verses 16-28.)

Does he think of the past? It is the record of God's faithful dealings with him: "You have held me by my right hand."

Does he think of the present? God is near: "I am continually with you."

Does he survey the future of his earthly existence? There shall be safe guiding all the way: "You shall guide me with Your counsel."

Does he survey the future after life is passed? Then shall be the Lord's presence: "You shall afterward receive me to glory."

Firm as a rock is the counsel and purpose of God with reference to the salvation and glory of His Church. Great is the difference between the designs, the intentions, the purposes of men, even the wisest and most powerful — and those of God. The former very frequently fail, break down, and come to an utter end — while the latter are invariably fulfilled.

The Book of Proverbs is full of this truth:
"A man's heart devises his way — but the Lord directs his steps."

"The lot is cast into the lot — but the whole disposing thereof is of the Lord."

"There are many devices in a man's heart — nevertheless the counsel of the Lord shall stand."

Even so elsewhere:
"He is of one mind, and who can turn Him?"

"What His soul desires, even that He does."

"The Lord brings the counsel of the heathen to nothing."

"He makes the devices of the people of no effect."

"The counsel of the Lord stands forever, the thoughts of His heart to all generations."

"All the inhabitants of the earth are reputed as nothing! He does according to His will in the army of Heaven and among the inhabitants of the earth; and none can stay His hand or say unto Him: What are You doing?"

That the purposes and schemes of man perpetually
fail, however carefully or skillfully devised, is plain to us
all.

A mighty tower is to be reared: it shall bring a great
name to its builders; it shall unite them together in one city;
it shall spread their fame far and wide. So the workmen
begin their task: brick upon brick, little by little, it soon
reaches a great height. But shall it be finished? Nay, the
tower of pride becomes Babel — the tower of confusion
and shame. For God ever brings low the proud and
haughty, so He confounds their language, and instead of the
builders being knit together, they are scattered abroad on
the face of the earth!

In all ages does God work in the same way:
you see it in the highest places,
you see it in the lowest places,
you see it in private families,
you see it in the affairs of nations.

Schemes are devised . . .
for the gratification of ambition,
for the increase of wealth,
for the indulgence of some evil passion —
yes, and for far better objects — to assist some friend
to provide against the day of adversity, or the like.

Yet in the providence of God it does not succeed, but
the object is rather hindered than furthered by the effort.

In the same way is it with plans that effect whole
communities. For months or years plans are nurtured for
the advancement of some secular or ecclesiastical power, to
place on a firm basis some doubtful title, or to raise to a

higher pitch of earthly glory some king or kingdom, some Church or Empire. But when the attempt is made, there is a total failure — matters have been miscalculated; things do not take the course expected; new elements come in that were not looked for; everything goes wrong — defeat comes instead of victory. This is aggravated by some fresh calamity, and the fruit of labor, and of efforts almost incalculable — is a harvest of ruin and desolation and woe.

Never perhaps has this been more evident than in the war between France and Germany. An Empire of late holding in its hands the destinies of Europe, going forth to a struggle with a neighboring power, in spite of the remonstrances of other nations — then in one single month losing almost everything — one vast army made captive, another army shut up so that it could never escape — the capital threatened, towns and villages burnt down or otherwise destroyed, the provision laid up for the winter season carried away for the use of hostile troops. Then have we been taught more clearly that man proposes, but God disposes, that neither king nor kingdom is saved by the multitude of an army, nor by all the power that man can summon to his aid!

But while human counsels frequently fail — the great I AM rules on high, and that which is in His heart and mind, moves on steadily to its glorious fulfillment. When the great book is fully written which shall contain the whole history of our globe and God's dealings with mankind — when we see revealed one man's prayer and another man's pride, and then trace how the hand of the Almighty has ever been uppermost, lifting up the humble and breaking down the high thoughts of the proud — sometimes working by His providence to fulfill what man has attempted, sometimes as plainly bringing it to nothing;

at the same time by means of all completing in the very best way His own designs — then how greatly will it exalt and glorify His own infinite wisdom, faithfulness, and power!

We read much, during the war to which I referred, of that strange mysterious man working out in his quiet room the plan of the campaign; sending here and there, by telegraphic wires, or by ready servants, by footmen, or by horsemen — messages to guide the generals under him; by a stroke of his pen, by a movement of his hand, directing armies at his will, moving as one man several hundreds of thousands of fighting men — and thus, beyond all expectation, bringing about a measure of success and victory seldom if ever before seen.

But look beyond him, and see Him who is the Only Wise God. Behold Him over His wide dominion controlling all things! His dominion extends not over a single portion of the earth — but over all lands, and over the wide domain of the universe. It reaches not the army of one nation, but every living man. It is exercised not for a few months, but from everlasting to everlasting.

His object is not to maintain the power or prestige of one kingdom, or to consolidate its various parts — but to set up His kingdom everywhere, to beat down the power of the great enemy, and to gather into one all things both in Heaven and earth, and to bind them fast together in Christ our Head.

Every view of this glorious design enhances our wonder and admiration.

Consider the mountains of difficulty that lay in the way of the accomplishment of God's plan of salvation — the mighty strength of evil, the craft of the Prince of Darkness, the enmity of human hearts, a world in rebellion against its Creator and ready to despise both His mercy and His justice.

Consider the central figure in whom and through whom the design is carried out: He is very God and very man — without sin and yet bearing in Himself the sin of the world — once dying yet evermore living — once counted the Nazarene, the Man of Sorrows, enduring the shame of a malefactor's death, and yet made higher than the angels, lifted up to the very throne of God, the Mediator, the High Priest, the Forerunner, the King, the Everlasting Savior of His people.

Consider the complex machinery employed — all the revolutions of kingdoms, all the events of private life, the preaching of the Word, and the prayers of the saints, the labors of God's workers, the evil deeds of the ungodly neutralized and overruled for good, the deaths of martyrs, the lives of those who walk in God's ways, the grace of the Divine Spirit, and the Providence of God working through all — so various are the agencies which He employs for fulfilling His counsels.

Consider also the everlasting felicity which this design will bring to countless souls. Two passages are closely allied: "He works all things after the counsel of His own will." And this will the highest good of his chosen ones: "All things work together for good to those who love God."

By and by shall we see fully manifested the everlasting good which He has wrought for His redeemed people. The purified spirit, the glorified body, the unfading inheritance, and the presence of the Lamb, with visions of Eternal Love as yet far beyond us — these will bring a joy that has neither limit nor end.

And this design cannot be frustrated — it is like the covenant, ordered in all things and sure. It is not dependent on the changing will of man, but on Him with whom is no variableness neither shadow of turning. It is firm and steadfast, and nothing can overturn it. Yes, more, it is advancing towards its completion.

Ages of preparation have passed away;
the Son of God has been manifested in the flesh;
the Gospel has been preached in almost every nation;
the oracles of Divine Wisdom have been made known
in two hundred languages;
myriads of souls have been turned from Satan unto
God.

On every side there is much to tell us that we may look for the time when the mystery of God, spoken of through bygone ages by patriarchs, prophets, and apostles, will be finished, and when the Son of God shall reign with His saints forever.

Let the consideration of the steadfastness of God's truth leave with us one or two lessons for our guidance.

1. Let the Christian be firm as a rock in the hope and rejoicing of the Gospel. True, in us there is everything to throw us back — we mourn our unfaithfulness, we confess with shame how little we rise to the height of our privileges, how little we have done to honor Him who has done all for us; our sins testify against us, our backslidings

are increased; yet is it still true, and true for us, that Christ Jesus came into the world to save sinners, that He will never reject any who truly turn to Him, that His arm is long enough and His heart is loving enough to rescue us from the mire of evil!

It is still true that the Good Shepherd will never lose one of His sheep, but will give them life eternal, and none shall pluck them out of His hand!

It is still true that He will sanctify and cleanse His Church and every member of it, and present it spotless and unblamable before the throne!

It is still true that He regards our humble confessions and accepts the breathing of contrite spirits, and that the sorrowful sighing of His prisoners enters into His ear and touches His heart.

Why then need we cast away our hope, or look downward in despondency and fear? Nay, rather let us afresh throw more wholly upon Him the burden of our salvation! Let us commit ourselves to Him, and believe that He will honor our confidence and fulfill our desires.

When Ruth learned by experience the kindness and good-will of Boaz — she came and laid herself down at his feet as he rested in the threshing-floor; and thus, by an act, very expressive in those days, manifested her desire to yield herself up to his care and affection. Nor did he refuse the charge, but undertook her cause and made her his own. Even thus may we by hearty reliance throw ourselves upon Him who is our near kinsman, and who will not let the matter drop, but will manifest in the gates of His Church that He claims us as His portion forever.

Neither let us fear for the changes that may come. We know not what is before us — but God knows, and that is enough. He knows, He will care, He will provide, He will protect.

If the world changes — He changes not. If health gives way, if a child or parent or a spouse dies, if losses in business come upon us — yet Jesus Christ is the same, the promises are the same, the purposes of heavenly love are the same, God Himself is the same.

"God is our refuge and strength, an ever-present help in times of trouble!" Psalm 46:1

God, and . . .
not blind fate,
not chance or luck,
not a kind of indefinite Providence,
not our good fortune,
not our courage,
not our determination.

No! God Himself is our refuge and strength, an ever-present help in times of trouble! The God of Jacob — so watchfully leading us, and preserving us from all evil; the Lord Almighty — He who has all the armies of Heaven and earth at His command — He is . . .
our refuge,
the hiding-place to which we can ever flee,
the stronghold from storm or foe, from fire or flood!

Yes, more, He is our strength, the Rock on which the heart may lean — the Holy Spirit strengthening the frailty of our nature by enabling us to lean wholly on our Father and our God.

Yes, more, He is our help. His hand stretched out to assist us whenever we turn to Him with the cry, "Give us help from trouble, for vain is the help of man."

Yes, more, an ever-present help! There is help always at hand. Many of those poor wounded soldiers in the war had dear ones at home who would gladly have run to their help; but they were far, far away. But God is nigh — so present, that but a sigh, a prayer — and He is by our very side.

Yes, more, help now — present in time as well as in space, when tomorrow may be too late. Yes, an hour lost, may lose all. But He gives immediate support, He is very close at hand, and very quick to support. Jesus never comes too late!

Why then be afraid? Why be too much disturbed though all things on earth are shaken? Rather let us add, with the Psalmist: "Therefore we will not fear, though the earth gives way and the mountains fall into the heart of the sea, though its waters roar and foam and the mountains quake with their surging. Nations are in uproar, kingdoms fall; He lifts his voice, the earth melts. The LORD Almighty is with us — the God of Jacob is our fortress!"

It was thus with a standard-bearer in Christ's Church, lately called away from us. In a letter addressed to the congregation from his dying bed, the late Rev. W.B. Mackenzie said: "They tell me that you want to hear some testimony to the sufficiency of my faith in Christ. I have preached to you for thirty-two years the Atonement of Christ, His perfect righteousness, and salvation through His blood. These truths are now my hope, my comfort, my stay. I believe that God's righteousness is mine, and that Christ's atonement is my perfect satisfaction for sin; and God's holy indwelling Spirit is my support and my life now. In this faith I have lived — and in this faith I die. I have nothing else, and I want no more. My faith is firm as a rock! I know whom I have believed, and am persuaded that He is able to keep that which I have committed to Him against that day. The time of my departure is at hand. I have fought the good fight, I have finished the race, I have kept the faith. Now there is in store for me the crown of righteousness, which the Lord, the righteous Judge, will award to me on that day — and not only to me, but also to all who have longed for his appearing!"

Let the Christian be firm as a rock in the defense and maintenance of God's truth.

Boldly to resist the soul-destroying errors that are abroad, and manfully to stand up for old truths is a matter most urgent at the present day. Hezekiah gives us a noble example: Men took the brazen serpent, and made an idol of it and worshiped it; but Hezekiah broke the idol in pieces, and called it Nehushtan — a piece of brass; and God blessed him in whatever he did.

On such foundational points, we must not be afraid to speak out plainly; we must not hesitate because many who teach error are kind and earnest, or even men of very holy and exemplary lives. Take heed not to be led away by the skeptical teaching that would cut out of Holy Scripture everything that makes it precious as a direct revelation from God of the way of salvation, and that would cast overboard that certainty of truth without which we can never rest our souls in peace upon its promises.

But while resisting error, we must also most diligently labor for the propagation of the truth.

In all our Sunday schools we need vigorous efforts to make the religious teaching more definite and heart searching, as well as to gather in the outcasts. We must second the efforts now made to increase very largely the sale or free distribution of good gospel literature. We must enter in by the open doors which are set before us — to preach Christ in the workshop, in the street, or in the home. There ought to be no drones in the hive, and no idlers in the vineyard — but all should be workers, laborers, helpers, soldiers — laboring, praying, toiling, fighting to make their influence felt on all sides, and to leave their mark on the world and the Church when they have left it. The great motive must ever be Christ's love. A few words of a hymn set forth the right principle we should ever strive to maintain:

> Am I a soldier of the cross,
> A follower of the Lamb?
> And shall I fear to own His cause,
> Or blush to speak His name?
>
> Must I be carried to the skies
> On flowery beds of ease,
> While others fought to win the prize,
> And sailed through bloody seas?
>
> Are there no foes for me to face?
> Must I not stem the flood?
> Is this vile world a friend to grace,
> To help me on to God?
>
> Sure I must fight if I would reign;

Increase my courage, Lord;
I'll bear the toil, endure the pain,
Supported by Your Word.

Your saints in all this glorious war
Shall conquer, though they die;
They see the triumph from afar,
By faith's discerning eye.

When that illustrious day shall rise,
And all Your armies shine
In robes of victory through the skies,
The glory shall be Thine!

"Therefore, my beloved brethren, be steadfast,
immovable, always abounding in the work of the Lord,
knowing that your toil is not in vain in the Lord!" 1
Corinthians 15:58

Christ's Blood More Precious than Gold!

"For you know that it was not with perishable things such as silver or gold that you were redeemed from the empty way of life handed down to you from your forefathers, but with the precious blood of Christ, a lamb without blemish or defect!" 1 Peter 1:18-19

How great is the price which has been paid for man's redemption! If a prisoner of war, shut up within the walls of some gloomy fortress, were to see a bag of gold sent for his ransom, by the Sovereign whom he had faithfully served — what thankfulness would fill his breast! But much more than this has been given for us. In tender compassion for our souls, no less a price has been paid by Christ than His own precious blood.

He saw us perishing in our sins;
He saw us in captivity to the Prince of Darkness;
He saw us tied fast by chains that we ourselves could never break
— and then He came to redeem us! He poured out upon the cross, the blood that was to be the means of our everlasting salvation.

Reader, how infinitely precious is this blood. Ever since the fall has God been reminding man of this truth.

Look at the blood of Abel's offering, which God accepted — while the offering of Cain was rejected.

Look at the blood of the Paschal lamb sprinkled upon the door posts of the Israelites, and which saved their firstborn from death.

Look at the streams of blood continually flowing from Jewish altars.

Look at the blood which the High Priest, once every year, on the great day of atonement, sprinkled before the mercy-seat.

Look at the blood with which Moses sprinkled both the book and all the people.

What were these, but so many voices by which God was telling men, in Old Testament times, of the value and the preciousness of the blood, which should hereafter be shed?

Look at that commemorative rite — that holy ordinance — which Christ instituted before His death, and which has ever since been so distinguishing a mark of Christ's Church. Consider how, throughout the last eighteen centuries, Christians have continually been meeting together to partake of that cup, of which Jesus said, "This is My blood of the New Covenant, which is shed for many for the remission of sin." Surely in this way God has ever been teaching His people the preciousness of the blood which was shed for our salvation.

It may be a profitable inquiry for us to make: "Why is this blood so infinitely precious?" I answer:

This blood is infinitely precious, because it is Divine. It is the blood of one who is man's Creator, "Perfect God —

and perfect man." "Equal to the Father as touching His Godhead, and inferior to the Father as touching His manhood." The prophet Zechariah speaks of the fountain of this blood which was hereafter to be opened: "In that day there shall be a fountain opened to the house of David and to the inhabitants of Jerusalem for sin and for impurity." (Zechariah 13.1.) But how shall that fountain be opened? Whose blood must be shed? Read verse 7. It is the fellow of the Lord Almighty — He who is one in essence, one in glory with the Eternal Father: "Awake, O sword, against my shepherd, and against the man that is my fellow, says the Lord Almighty."

Oh, ponder well this deep and mysterious truth. Little can we fathom it! Yet was it God Incarnate — God in our nature — the Eternal Word made flesh — who died for man's salvation How marvelous it was!

His own hand had fashioned the very wood upon which He was nailed!

He Himself gave breath to the very men who cried out, "Away with Him, away with Him, crucify Him!"

It was His power which gave strength and nerve to the arm which pierced His side with the cruel spear!

Yes! the Creator and Preserver of man — the King of kings and Lord of lords, He before whom angels worshiped, crying, "Holy, holy, holy, Lord God Almighty!" — He it was who suffered a shameful and cruel death at the hands of His own creatures!

What a mystery of love!

It is written in Psalm 116, "Precious in the sight of the Lord is the death of His saints." How infinitely precious then must be the blood-shedding of His own dear Son! What infinite efficacy must that blood possess as the ransom for our souls!

Again, this blood is also precious because it is pure and holy.

Christ was "Holy, harmless, undefiled, and separate from sinners." (Hebrews 7:26.) As it was needful that the lamb offered as the daily sacrifice in the temple must be without blemish — so it was necessary that Jesus should be free from the least taint of evil — and so He was. He mingled with sinners at every turn — He mingled with them in the temple and in the synagogue, in their streets and in their homes. It was thrown in His teeth that He was "the friend of publicans and sinners."

On another occasion it was brought as a charge against Him: "This man receives sinners, and eats with them!" (Luke 15.2.) The charge was true — He loved to go among sinners that He might save and help them — yet all the while not the shadow of pollution ever defiled His pure and holy character. He could appeal to His foes, and say, "Which of you convinces Me of sin?"

Listen also to the various testimonies given to His perfect sinlessness:

Hear the witness of those who were His most intimate companions, who had been with Him at all seasons: Peter declares that He was a "Lamb without blemish and without spot" (1 Peter 1:20); and again, "He did no sin, neither was deceit found in His mouth." John, who lay on His bosom, declares, "You know that He was manifested to take away our sins — and in Him was no sin." (1 John 3:5.)

Hear the witness of His enemies — those who shared in the guilt of His crucifixion: Pilate declares, "I find in Him no fault at all!" And again, "I am innocent of the blood of this innocent man!" Judas, the traitor, declares, "I have sinned in that I have betrayed the innocent blood." The Centurion at the cross declares, "Certainly this was a righteous man!"

The Devils too confessed the innocence of the Savior, for they cried, "We know You who You are — the Holy One of God."

And the Father Himself bore witness to it, when He declared, at His Baptism, "This is my beloved Son in whom I am well pleased."

Here we have friends and enemies, devils and God Himself — all uniting their witness to the perfect holiness of Christ. Surely then this blood must be precious.

Here is another element of its unfailing efficacy: it is the blood of One who, as man's substitute, as man's representative, offered a perfect and sinless obedience to the Law which man had broken.

Again this blood is precious because it is the pledge and expression of infinite compassion and love.

The very least gift is valued if it comes as the fruit of genuine love; and surely nothing was ever such a proof of love — a love so incomprehensible, so amazing — as the blood of Christ.

By three steps we may learn to know a little of the love of Christ, which surpasses knowledge:

1. His words. Oh, what bright glimpses of the love which dwelt in Christ's heart may we gain — if we listen to the words which fell from His lips! Hear but a few.

"Come unto Me, all who labor and are heavy laden, and I will give you rest." (Matthew 11.28.)

"Are not five sparrows sold for two farthings, and not one of them is forgotten before God. But even the very hairs of your head are all numbered. Fear not therefore — you are of more value than many sparrows." (Luke 12.6, 7.)

"The Son of man has come to seek and to save that which was lost." (Luke 19.10.)

"Him that comes to Me I will never cast out." (John 6.37.)

"If any man thirsts, let him come unto Me and drink." (John 7.37.)

"I am the good Shepherd — the good Shepherd gives His life for the sheep." (John 10.11.)

"As the Father has loved Me, so have I loved you." (John 15.9.)

Oh, what beams from the Sun of Righteousness are these gracious words! Well may they dispel every doubt and fear from the soul that seeks Him.

2. Rise a step higher. Look at Christ's tears. Christ had but one day of triumph during His thirty-three years' sojourn upon earth. It was the day when He entered Jerusalem, shortly before His death, amidst the Hosannas of the multitude: "The multitude that went before, and that followed, cried, saying, Hosanna to the Son of David! Blessed is He who comes in the name of the Lord; Hosanna in the highest." (Matthew 21.9.) On that day did Jesus weep. "He beheld the city and wept over it." (Luke 19.41.)

Oh, what a deep well of compassion in the Savior's heart do those tears reveal! If you saw a father weeping before he took the rod to punish a rebellious child — would you not say the father had a deep love for the child, whom he felt compelled to punish? So when we see Christ weeping before He sent the scourge of the Roman army to destroy the city which He loved — must we not own the greatness of His pity and compassion?

Yes, those tears tell us how Jesus pitied the souls of those who were perishing in their sins — and He is still the same. Every tear He shed assures us that He still yearns over the guilty and the lost. Oh, how should the tears of Christ melt and subdue our proud and stony hearts! How ought they to quicken us to a true and hearty repentance!

3. Rise a step higher. His precious blood. Christ's words reveal His love, still more His tears — but most of all, the blood which He shed.

When the Jews saw the tears which Jesus shed at the tomb of Lazarus His friend, they rightly judged when they said, "Behold how He loved him!" When we see the drops of precious blood falling on Calvary, when we see the blood flowing from His pierced temples, from His wounded hands and feet and side, well may we say, "Behold, how He loved us!"

Bear in mind that the suffering in body, the shame and the scoffing, were but the least part of that which He endured for our sake. His holy soul was burdened with the weight of man's transgression. How agonizing was the conflict, when thrice He prayed in the garden, that if it were possible the cup might pass from Him! How great was the inner darkness of His soul, when on the cross there arose that exceeding great and bitter cry, "My God, my God! Why have You forsaken Me!"

It has been said, "Christ received into His own bosom every arrow of God's quiver, and every one dipped in the poison of the curse!" Here then is love. In the blood of the cross, we find the proof of such love as man never before could conceive: "Greater love has no man than this, that a man lay down his life for his friends." (John 15:13.)

Again: the blood of Christ is precious because it has power to cleanse from all guilt. How great is man's need of cleansing and forgiveness! Consider the vast amount of guilt that lies at the door of every unpardoned sinner. Take the life of any one who is yet a stranger to God; judge his life in the light of God's holy law, and who can tell how great the debt — how countless the iniquities of such a one?

Begin with acts of positive disobedience — dishonest gains, deceits, secret sins which the world knows nothing of — such things as even natural conscience will reprove. Add to these, sins of the tongue — lying words, profane words, angry words, murmuring words, vain and foolish words, remembering the solemn declaration of Christ,

"Truly I say unto you, that for every idle word that men shall speak, they shall give account thereof in the day of judgment." (Matthew 12.36.) Add to these, multitudes of unhallowed thoughts and imaginations, unchaste and unholy desires, crowds of sinful and vain thoughts, as many as the motes in the sunbeam, remembering again the Word of God: "The thought of foolishness is sin." (Proverbs 24.9.) Add all these together, and who can count their number?

I have seen a strange list, the catalogue of the crimes of a man who was executed at Norfolk Island, with the punishment he received for each offence, and this list was between two and three yards in length — but what was this compared to the catalogue of each man's transgressions against the Most High? We might almost say that this catalogue, written out by the hand of God, would reach from earth to Heaven, applying the words of Ezra: "Our iniquities are increased over our head, and our trespass is grown up into the heavens."

Perhaps, however, we gain a more impressive view of this truth if we regard the life of an unconverted man as one continuous sin. What was the life of the younger son, in the parable given in Luke 15, while he remained in the far country? Was not every moment a moment of rebellion and ingratitude, and therefore one continuous sin? No doubt there were hours of grosser iniquity — hours when he plunged deeper into excess — yet was not his whole life, and every moment of it, sinful and rebellious?

Now it is just so with every sinner, until he has yielded to the merciful call of God — until he has come home as a penitent to the Father's house. Each moment of his life he is plainly disregarding the first and great commandment: "You shall love the Lord your God with all your heart, with all your soul and with all your might." What moment, therefore, is he not disobeying God and therefore sinning against Him?

Oh, careless, thoughtless sinner! Be assured of this — your life is one long continued sin, extending from your birth to this very moment. Wherever you may be — in the house of God, or in the house of business, in the field, or walking by the way-side, in some scene of worldly dissipation, or by your own fireside; whatever you may be doing — eating or drinking, talking or sleeping, rising in the morning or going to rest at night, yes, even going through a routine of worship, reading your accustomed chapter of Scripture, or repeating certain forms of prayer — yet until you return to God, with hearty and sincere repentance, still, every moment you are sinning against Him.

But take the life of the child of God, and see even here how much sin there is that needs the constant exercise of pardoning mercy.

Look at it in this light: put the cleanest linen beside the freshly driven snow — how soiled, how discolored does it appear! So compare the life of the holiest child of God with the life of Christ. Consider . . .

His meekness,
His purity and holiness,
His prayerfulness,
His self-denial,
His constant zeal in His Father's work,
His tender compassion both for the bodies and the souls of men

— and then side by side with this put the life of the believer. How great is the contrast! In the life of the believer —

how much evil is mingled with the good!

How much is of the earth, earthy!

How much deadness and coldness of heart!

How much selfishness and sloth!

How much regard to present appearances, rather than the will of God!

How many backslidings!

How many wanderings in prayer!

How many neglects of duty!

How many lost opportunities of usefulness!

Truly, the believer has need to echo the lament of Isaiah the prophet: "We are all as an unclean thing, and all our righteousnesses are as filthy rags! All of us wither like a leaf, and our iniquities, like the wind, take us away!" (Isaiah 64:6.)

Now in sight of all this amount of guilt, both on the part of the unconverted man and on that of the child of God — God offers, in every case, a perfect, everlasting forgiveness, through the blood of His Son.

The promise of Isaiah is full and free: "Come now, and let us reason together, says the Lord: Though your sins are like scarlet, I will make them as white as snow. Though they are red like crimson — I will make them as white as wool!" (Isaiah 1:18.)

But the anxious soul, beholding the justice and strictness of God's law, is ready to ask: What can remove guilt so great as mine? What can take away these ark blots that have defiled my life?

John gives us the answer, in that oft quoted declaration: "If we walk in the light, as He is in the light, we have fellowship one with another, and the blood of Jesus Christ, His Son, cleanses us from all sin!"

Paul again has said: "In whom we have redemption through His blood, the forgiveness of sins, according to the riches of His grace." (Ephesians 1:7.)

Reader, be assured of this — there is a power and efficacy in the blood of the Cross that can enable the guiltiest and vilest sinner to stand spotless in the sight of a holy God — a power that can pacify the most distressed and burdened conscience.

But perhaps there may be in your case, some peculiarity, some special aggravations of your guilt — so that you may imagine pardon to be next to impossible for you. There may be the remembrance of some dark hour of iniquity that rises up, offtimes like a thick cloud, to hide from you the light of God's countenance. Your constant failures, your broken resolutions, your sad lack of repentance and faith and love — may sorely pain and grieve you. Do not yield to the voice of the Tempter, who would persuade you to cast away your confidence in the blood of sprinkling.

Is your sin a grief and a burden to you?

Do you wish to forsake it and walk before God in newness of life?

Do you endeavor to watch and pray against it?

Then doubt not for a single moment there is pardon for you. Remember Luther's dream: It seemed to him, that the Tempter brought before him the sins with which he was chargeable in a single day. One by one he wrote them all out before him, and then asked him how such a one as he could be saved? Luther owned them all — but wrote at the close of the long, dark catalogue, "The blood of Jesus Christ cleanses us from all sin."

The blood of Christ is also precious, because it brings the sinner near to God. It is written, "Now in Christ Jesus you who once were afar off are made near by the blood of Christ." (Ephesians 2:13.)

Through the blood of Christ, not only is sin forever removed — but the sinner is received and welcomed as a dear child! Not now is he the pardoned rebel — not the hired servant, but the child very near to the Father's heart. Once the sinner stood afar off; once he was ready to cry out, "Depart from me, for I am a sinful man, O Lord!" Once he shrank with fear from the presence of One whose holiness condemned his sin!

But now, how changed are his feelings! The blood of Jesus has won the heart for God.

Fear of God is gone — love to God has taken its place.

Now he delights to draw near to the throne of grace.

Now he loves to ponder the gracious promises which his Father has given him.

Now he desires to walk closely with God, and to obey His commandments. As a dear child can he now cry,

"Abba, Father!" He can rest all his cares and sorrows upon a Father's heart. Whatever may befall him during his earthly pilgrimage, he can still rejoice that God is near to him as a reconciled Father.

"So near, so very near to God!
I cannot nearer be,
For in the person of His Son,
I am as near as He.

"So dear, so very dear to God!
I cannot dearer be,
For the love with which He loves His son,
Such is His love to me."

Lastly, the blood is precious because it brings the sinner safely to glory. Here is the final blessing, here is the full joy purchased for the sinner by the blood of Christ — it brings him safe to the shores of the heavenly Canaan.

What that world will be, remains as yet unrevealed to us. What the brightness and glory of that city of the living God, where there is no need of the sun or moon to lighten it; what the joyful rest of that home, where the door is forever shut against sin, and fear, and care, and temptation, and suffering, and death — no heart can conceive or tongue describe!

Reader, picture to yourself that great assembly and Church of the first-born. See the whole family gathered together around the throne. See the many who come from the North and from the South, from the East and from the West — of every kindred and nation and people and tongue. See the perfect holiness in which they shine. See the unclouded glory which belongs to them. See the Lamb

Himself in the midst, leading them to living fountains of waters, still opening to them fresh streams of everlasting bliss. Hear the anthem of redeeming love, which arises from every tongue: "Salvation to our God who sits upon the throne, and unto the Lamb!"

Then inquire, "Why are they here? Who are these arrayed in white robes, and where did they come from?"

An angel shall give the answer. "These are those who came out of great tribulation, and have washed their robes, and made them white in the blood of the lamb. Therefore are they before the throne of God, and serve him day and night in his temple!" (Rev. 7:14, 15.)

Notice the word "therefore." Here is the one single reason that the glorious company of the redeemed could stand before the throne: they had washed away their sins in the Savior's blood. Every one will rejoice to confess it — "All this glory, my mansion, my inheritance, my crown, my kingdom — all has been won for me by Jesus! It is the gift of His wondrous love — it is the purchase of His precious blood!"

I ask, therefore, is not this blood precious? Remember whose blood it is: that of the Eternal Son of God. Remember how pure and holy was the character of Him who shed it. Remember it is the gift of a love far beyond all our thoughts. Think . . .
how many a guilty conscience it has relieved,
how many a weary heart it has comforted,
how many a bright hope of glory it has given.

Think what multitudes who once were perishing in the mire of sin — near to Hell, near to eternal ruin — it has cleansed, purified, and brought to everlasting salvation.

Ob, may the eternal Spirit reveal these things to us! It is His work alone to do it. May He convince us of our manifold and great iniquities! May He lead us truly, deeply, solemnly, to feel the mighty power of that blood, by which they can be completely and forever removed!

Let me close with a few words of counsel suggested by this subject.

Beware of the guilt and danger of neglecting this precious blood! This is the greatest act of disobedience. The first and great commandment of the law was, "You shall love the Lord your God with all your heart, with all your soul, and with all your strength." The great commandment of the Gospel is that we should believe in Christ: "This is His commandment — That we should believe on the name of His Son Jesus Christ." (1 John 3:23.) Without obedience to this, no duty can be acceptable to God. Our very first act of acceptable obedience, must be believing in Christ — washing away our sins in His most precious blood.

Again, is it not the deepest ingratitude to neglect this blood? Has the Son of God come down from Heaven? Has He taken our nature that He might bear the curse which belonged to us? Has He died in suffering, in shame, upon the cross? Has He, at such a cost, opened a fountain for the cleansing of our souls? And is it no ingratitude to refuse to go to it? Is it no ingratitude to turn from His cross, and to refuse His offered mercy?

Be sure of this — no love was ever so great as that of Christ, in the blood which He shed for sinners — and no ingratitude can be so great as making light of His salvation.

Beware too of the danger of neglecting this blood. What safety is there for a single moment, except beneath its shelter? If the Israelite had neglected to sprinkle the lintel and door-posts of his dwelling with the blood of the paschal lamb, the destroying angel would have entered and smitten his first-born. And if the sinner neglects to have his heart and conscience sprinkled by faith with the blood of Christ, assuredly the angel of justice will not spare him. There can be no salvation — none whatever — for those who will not take it through the blood of Christ.

Let every one who desires salvation, take up his dwelling-place near to this Fountain opened for sin and impurity. To every one who asks the way to Zion — who longs for a full and everlasting forgiveness — I would give a short and plain direction. It is that given by Elisha to the Syrian leper: "Wash, and be clean!"

Are you just waking from the sleep of sin — just discovering for the first time how great is your guilt before a just and holy God? The message is for you. Jesus has died — the fountain is open — the promise is free. "Whoever shall call on the name of the Lord shall be saved!" Go in faith, with the prayer, "Wash me, and I shall be whiter than snow!" The answer shall come: "Son, or daughter, be of good cheer, your sins be forgiven!"

Are you a backslider? Have you turned away from Christ? Do you feel as if such sin could never be pardoned? Yet despair not. It is true you have brought dishonor upon the name of Christ; you have brought up an evil report of the good land; you have in fact said to those around you, "I have tried the world, and I have tried Christ — and the world is the best master." Still, once again, turn to Christ — like Peter, return to Him in true penitence and faith. His blood shall cleanse your sin — even your's. Only try it, and the promise shall be fulfilled to you: "I will heal their backslidings, I will love them freely, for my anger is turned away from them." (Hosea 14:4.)

Are you a believer, clinging only to Jesus, and yet often distressed on account of your manifold sins and infirmities? Here is your safety, here is your comfort — a continual resort to this Open Fountain. Like Naaman, in Jordan, wash seven times — yes, seventy times seven. This fountain is the only place on earth where sin and doubt and fear die — and where grace and holiness and love thrive and grow.

When the remembrance of sin comes over you like a dark shadow, then go to the fountain — wash and be clean! When you kneel down at the mercy-seat and desire with confidence to draw near to God — then wash and be clean! (Hebrews 10.19-22.) When you feel how imperfect and defiled have been your prayers, how every Sabbath service has been mingled with sin; when you feel that such worship cannot be accepted — again go to the fountain: wash and be clean! When the closing hour draws near, and face to face you meet the King of terrors; when your last chapter has been read, when you have borne your last testimony for the Savior whom you love — still abide by the fountain. Bathed in its precious waters, let your spirit ascend to your Father in Heaven. Entering your eternal rest, you shall join more fully in the song of the redeemed, which you have learned to sing here on earth: "Unto Him who loved us, and washed us from our sins in His own blood, and has made us kings and priests unto God and His Father — to Him be glory and dominion forever and ever! Amen." (Rev. 1:5, 6.)

Let the believer live in constant remembrance of the price which has been paid for his redemption.

Believer, did Jesus give His precious blood for you, to save you from Hell and damnation, to give you peace of conscience, to make you a child of God and an heir of eternal glory — then what will you withhold from Him? Oh, surrender yourself wholly, unreservedly to His service! "You are bought with a price, therefore glorify God in your body and in your spirit, which are God's." (1 Corinthians 6.20.)

Oh, think of the debt of love you owe, and endeavor to make some return for it, by laying yourself and all you have at His feet. Time, talents, influence, wealth — freely yield to the Savior who has bought you! Employ every member of your body as an instrument of righteousness for Him. The hand, the foot, the eye, the ear, the tongue, all may be used for His glory, and to promote the extension of His kingdom. Above all things, live daily, hourly, as in the sight of God; adorn your profession by a very loving, holy, prayerful, Christ-like life. Abide in Christ by faith. Rely upon him every hour for fresh supplies of grace, for fresh anointings of his quickening, sanctifying spirit. Look forward to his appearing: "Yet a little while, and He who shall come will come, and will not tarry." (Hebrews 10.37.)

The Upward Glance!

Year by year the Jewish pilgrims were accustomed to go up to Jerusalem from the various towns and villages of Judea and Galilee. As their annual feasts came around, they went up in bands and companies to the city of Zion, which they loved; and many a cheerful song did they chant along their way: the fifteen Psalms, from the 120th to the 134th, which are called songs of degrees or ascents, were especially used on these occasions. Thus they sang together: "Our feet shall stand within your gates, O Jerusalem! Pray for the peace of Jerusalem — they still prosper that love you. Peace be within your walls, and prosperity within your palaces. Those who trust in the Lord shall be as Mount Zion, which cannot be removed, but abides forever. Unto You lift I up my eyes, O You that dwell in the heavens."

We, like them, are on a journey Zionward. We have our pilgrimage to make to the dwelling place of our God. And we too need to go forth along our way with a song of confidence and hope and gladness.

And where shall we find one more suited for us than the words of the 123rd Psalm, which tell us where we must turn for all strength and consolation? Let coming years bring to us what they may, let their days be bright with almost unmingled prosperity, or darkened by clouds of sorrow and bitter anguish — yet these words tell of One who will never fail us — of a Friend and Helper who from His high and lofty throne regards with tenderest affection all those who make Him their Refuge and their Trust.

"Unto You will I lift up my eyes, O You that dwell in the heavens."

We may take these words as expressing the dawning of hope in the awakened soul. The Spirit awakens the sinner to see his true position. He is aroused to discover his imminent peril. Various are the means which that mighty Worker employs in this most needful work. Sometimes it is by a solemn appeal from the Sanctuary, sometimes by the death of a friend, or through a season of sickness; sometimes it is by means of some trivial incident. The late Lord Haddo cast a glance at the clothes which he had just taken off. The Spirit suggested the thought: "How soon must I lay aside this garment of mortality! How soon must I be unclothed of this frail body, and enter the presence of my Judge! Eternity comes on apace, and I am yet unprepared to meet it!" Thus began that blessed change which was soon manifested in his whole life and conduct.

But whatever be the instrument employed to touch the conscience and arrest the sinner, usually there follows for a time exceeding sorrow on account of his sin. What but sin — sin — sin everywhere in the past life? What but hardness and impenitence and unbelief is felt within the heart?

How was it with the one who went up into the temple to pray? He stands afar off, afar from the holy place, afar from the other worshipers, for he knows full well how far his life has been spent from God. Yes, more than this, he dares not look upward: "He would not lift up so much as his eyes to Heaven." The proud Pharisee fearlessly lifted up eyes and hands and face toward God, trusting in all the good deeds of which he boasts — but not so the humbled publican. It was as if he would say, "How dare I look up to that holy Being whom I have so long provoked to anger? How dare I look upward to that holy Heaven, where nothing impure can enter, which is the home of saints, and of the holy angels? And what is my plea? I dare say nothing, like this Pharisee, of that I have not done — for all evil have I wrought. I dare say nothing of that I have done. I dare not say that I have fasted, or prayed, or given tithes, for I have done neither the one nor the other. One thing I am — a sinner. One thing alone can meet my case — free and undeserved mercy. God be merciful to me, a sinner!"

But the Spirit can comfort as well as convict. He comes and darts a ray of hope into the dark and cheerless soul. He brings right home to the heart some gracious invitation or promise.

Then the soul bowed down with sin, with fear, with distress — ventures to look up. The eye hitherto downcast and moistened with many a tear — is turned heaven-ward. There is a looking upward, though with trembling. And what does the sinner now behold?

A God of vengeance — a God ready to cast upon him the hot thunderbolts of His fiery wrath? Nay, far otherwise.

He beholds a pitiful Father ready to forgive, bending over him in love and compassion.

He beholds a tender Shepherd waiting to restore him to the fold.

He beholds an all-wise Physician, ready to pour in the balm of Gilead for every wound.

He beholds a great High Priest, the one who once bore his sin on the cross of Calvary, now pleading for him before the throne.

He beholds a great and glorious Savior, ready to lift him up from all the guilt and dominion and degradation of sin — to a mansion of never-ending bliss!

Most earnestly would I beseech you, dear reader, if by grace you have been led to know something of your sin and danger — to look upwards to that faithful and mighty Redeemer, who is near to save and bless you. Tarry no longer — wait not until a more convenient season. Let nothing hinder you. Hide not yourself in the dark gloomy cellar of unbelief. Look not with too absorbing thought on the evil you have done — so that you cannot look to Him who will deliver you from it.

The bitten Israelite might have looked long at his wound before he would have found a cure — but an upward glance at the brazen serpent brought to him healing and life. Remember the old saying of the godly McCheyne: "For one look at yourself — take ten looks at Christ!"

And do you need a sure plea to carry with you to the mercy-seat?

Let it be this: "For Your Name's sake." Perhaps you cannot find any reason why God should save one so vile or so unworthy as yourself. You look within and without, and you say, "I can see no good thing that I can bring to God." Well, that is true. Yet is there hope. Plead the grace that there is in God — and not anything in yourself. "For Your Name's sake, O Lord, pardon my iniquity — for it is great."

I ask it for Your mercy's sake — O Lord, magnify that full ocean of mercy and love which is in Your breast.

I ask it for Your truth's sake — Your word, Your promise, Your oath, is passed that none shall seek Your face in vain. You can not deceive nor disappoint me.

I ask it for Your work's sake. I plead with You, that great work You have accomplished in the death of Your Son; that full atoning sacrifice and satisfaction which He has wrought in accordance with Your will.

Thus plead, and your plea cannot but succeed.

Ah, wherefore do I ever doubt?
You will never cast me out:
A helpless soul that comes to Thee,
With only sin and misery.

But we learn also in this passage to rise above the fear of man. It has been supposed that Nehemiah was the writer of the 123rd Psalm. Scornful foes were about him, and strove to impede the work he had in hand. Sanballat and Tobiah mocked him. They said, "What are these feeble Jews doing? That which they build, even a fox shall break down their stone wall." Thus he was cast down and troubled. "Our soul is exceedingly filled with the scorning of those that are at ease, and with the contempt of the proud."

But what is this faithful man's resource? He turns away from man. He looks away from the region of earth altogether. He remembers that One dwells on high who is mightier than all the children of men. He knows that if Jehovah is on his side — it matters not though ten thousands of the people set themselves against him round about. What though the Ammonite and Arabian conspire against us — we will work, we will watch, and we will pray. "Unto you lift I up my eyes, O You that dwell in the heavens."

It is well to take hold of this precious thought, that we be not turned aside by the frown or the reproach of our fellow-men. Be not daunted by anything that may be said or done against you for the Master's sake. Hold not back from an open confession of your allegiance, from reproving sin, from fighting the Lord's battles. If you are Christ's, those who are with you are more than those who are against you. If you have man's frown — you have God's favor. If you have the world's rebuke — you have Christ's approbation.

Yes, and may not these very trials be the very discipline you need? May they not lead you the closer to the great Friend? "None but God can tell how much good, unkind looks have done me; for times without number they have led me to the footstool of Him who is all kindness and love." Such was the experience of a devoted Christian lady. And why may it not be your own?

Man may trouble or distress me,
'Twill but drive me to Your breast;
Life with trials hard may press me,
Heaven will bring me sweeter rest.

We have here again the attitude of genuine, fervent, expectant prayer.

True spiritual prayer is often accompanied by the lifting up of the bodily eye, and is frequently spoken of as the lifting up of the eye of the soul. Jesus, when He prayed, "lifted up His eyes to Heaven, and said, Father, the hour has come — glorify Your Son, that Your Son also may glorify You." And in the Psalms we have perpetually the same idea. "My eyes are ever toward the Lord; for He shall pluck my feet out of the net." "I will lift up my eyes unto the hills, from whence comes my help. My help comes from the Lord, who made Heaven and earth."

In the 141st Psalm, we have a picture of the most hopeless condition possible, looking at it merely from a human point of view. It is as if a man were not only sick, but dead; not only dead, but buried; not only buried, but his bones dry and cast out of the grave — or as a tree hewn in pieces by the axe. Yet with prayer comes hope. "Our bones are scattered at the grave's mouth, as when one cuts and cleaves wood upon the earth. But my eyes are unto You, O God the Lord! In You is my trust, leave not my soul destitute."

Such is true prayer: the inner look of the soul upward

—

The upward glancing of the eye,
When none but God is near.

Reader, do you know anything of this? There may be the kneeling posture in church, or in the closet — there may be the utmost gravity and seriousness of manner — there may be all the outward form of devotion — there may be many words, and suitable words uttered by the lip — but what do you know of the looking of the soul heavenward? It is this which constitutes true prayer; it is this which God reckons as worshiping Him in Spirit and in truth. And wherever this is found, it is the fruit of God's Spirit working within the heart. It is the fountain of living water, springing upwards towards its source in holy desires and heavenly aspirations. It is the Holy Spirit lifting up the soul above its own natural earthliness to the God of the Spirits of all flesh.

Too many, alas, seldom have a desire or a thought heavenward. Their eye is fixed on earth. Their heart is wholly absorbed in the things of time. They dig their own grave — and then go and live in it all their days. They are so busied in the cares and pursuits of the moment, that they strive not to seek for an eternal portion above.

But if this is the case with any reader, what must needs be the outcome? If your heart is not above — can you expect your treasure there? If you send no messenger beforehand — no prayer, no earnest desire — can you look for an eternal and glorious home prepared for you? Nay, it cannot be. The final scene will usher you into an eternity where for you all will be dark indeed; the loss of all in which once you gloried — the midnight blackness of everlasting despair.

But with many readers it may be otherwise. You have known the value of prayer. You have learned the way to the mercy-seat. Amidst all the evil that still cleaves to you, your spirit from time to time can wing its way upward, and hold communion with the skies. Oh, then, I beseech you, stir up the grace which has thus been given to you! Trade diligently with this talent committed to your charge. Cultivate the habit of instant and believing prayer. Let your daily round of work and duty be hallowed by frequent aspirations wafted heavenward. As you walk to and fro along the oft trodden path that leads to your place of business, as you take your accustomed stroll after the day's toil, or as you go to visit a friend, or to purchase some necessary article for the needs of your household — why not dart upward, the arrow of earnest desire? Why not turn into prayer, some promise of Holy Scripture, some message from the pulpit, some sorrow or anxiety that may be weighing upon you? Why need there be an hour in the day in which you do not thus experience the lightening of some grief, or the bestowal of some spiritual blessing from above? It needs but a moment for a petition to ascend from the altar of your heart, to the ear of your Father in Heaven! "Pray without ceasing!" 1 Thessalonians 5:17. And be assured that such prayer is never lost. It is communion and merchandise of the most enriching character.

Many a merchant of late has sent across the ocean a message by the electric wires, that has involved very considerable expense, and yet the return has far outweighed the cost of its transmission. But here is a means of communication between us and the upper world, which is perfectly free and accessible to all such as will humbly and earnestly use it. And who can say how great may be the return?

Only let there be a close walk with God: only let prayer be a reality, your objects of petition distinctly defined, your reliance placed sincerely in the mediation of the Well-beloved, and your hearts kept in tune by the Spirit of prayer — and who shall count the gains which you may anticipate?

May you not look for a more satisfying enjoyment of the things of God? If the well of living water within the heart is deepened; if grace works mightily in casting out the old soil which hinders the up-springing of the Divine life; if there is a greater relish for the Word of truth, and the ordinances of the Lord's house — surely the gain will not be slight.

May you not also look for fresh doors of usefulness to be opened, and a richer blessing to rest on your effort for the welfare of others? If you would have wisdom to guide you in your plans for doing good, if you would have those plans crowned with success, if you would see one here and another there, benefitted by the words that you speak to them in the Master's name — you must move in an atmosphere of prayer, you must look upward for a zealous and child-like spirit, you must ask for a prepared heart in those to whom you minister, you must follow with fervent supplication whatever you have attempted to do.

May you not thus also meet in quiet resignation to the will of God, the inevitable changes and trials that may come upon you as time goes on? Temptations must be overcome, trials must be manfully borne, labors must be undertaken from which sometimes the flesh shrinks back; you must stand fast in positions of danger, and not fail in the duties that may then be incumbent upon you — and how can all this be?

A midshipman was climbing the mast for the first time: he grew dizzy, and ready to fall be cried out, "What shall I do?" "Keep looking up and you can do anything!" was the answer the captain gave.

Reader, take home the lesson: "Keep looking up, and you can do anything." You can stand fast in peril, you can endure toil and difficulty, you can meet with cheerful submission the sorrows that await you in the future, you can triumph even in the hour of your last agony — if only your eye is fixed on Jesus, your heavenly Intercessor, your everlasting Friend.

Thus also may we discern a door of hope amidst the thickening strife of these latter days. What fresh assaults, in various quarters have been made on the Church of Christ! What fresh advances have been made by the enemies of pure Scriptural truth! And within her gates, what a sad lack of zeal and energy! What a crying need for more plain preaching of the Word of God — the only food that can nourish the souls of her children. And in this our necessity, we must not despair: we must not give way to unavailing regrets. We must use all pains-taking diligence to counteract the evil, and promote that which is good. We must be quickened in our zeal by the remembrance of those that have gone before us, and having fought the good fight, have entered into their rest.

Oh, let us be ready to fill up the gap made by the loss of faithful men as one by one they are taken from the midst of us! Yet having done all that is in the power of our hand, we must look upwards to Him who alone can effectually support us, and who can do that we cannot do. We must look above all human power, to Him who reigns supreme over all things, both in Heaven and earth. He has means at His disposal, whereby He can easily frustrate every evil design, and bring near His salvation to those who are perishing for lack of knowledge. And for this we must daily pray. It is thus that the eye uplifted to Heaven brings near the blessing and the deliverance.

The Eternal Spirit of the living God, is that required above all things. By His power whatever foes beset us can easily be scattered. By the same power, the bread of Heaven can be brought near to multitudes of famishing souls, that they may be strong and joyful in the Lord's salvation.

And for this we will plead.

"Arise, O Lord, let Your enemies be scattered, and let them that hate You flee before You! Except the Lord keep the city the watchman wakes but in vain. Turn us then, O Lord God Almighty, cause Your face to shine, and we shall be saved.

It is well distinctly to set before us the encouraging truth, that "the upward glance" can never be in vain. For remember if man's eye be upward, God's eye is downward. The eye of Jehovah meets the eye of the humble trustful believer.

Side by side ought we to place the two thoughts: man's eye upward to God — God's eye turned toward man. On the one side: "Unto You I lift up my eyes." "Our eyes are unto You." and similar passages. On the other: "The eyes of the Lord are over the righteous, and His ears are open toward their prayer." "Behold the eye of the Lord is upon those who fear Him, upon those who hope in His mercy." Here we have the eye of the child looking for help to a compassionate Father, and the Father beholding His child with the tenderest love, and with an ear open to every petition.

Even if an earthly parent saw his child casting an imploring look toward him for some necessary aid, would he despise that glance? Would he not run in a moment to support him? And shall our Father in Heaven behold unmoved the eye of earnest longing and expectation fixed upon Him?

Remember also the mighty power of Him with whom we have to do. He dwells in Heaven as King of kings and Lord of lords. He has made Heaven and earth, and preserves all things by His ever-present care. To Him all the inhabitants of earth are reputed as nothing. He does according to His will in the army of Heaven, and among the inhabitants of earth.

And as He has power, so will He surely fulfill all His gracious purposes and counsels. Calmly He sits above the water floods, surveying all that is passing here below — all the shaking of Nations and of Churches and of Systems, all the noise and strife of political agitation — and through all, and by means of all carrying out His own great designs, and perfecting the living temple which He is building for His own glory. He will never forget His own Church. He will never permit the unruly wills of sinful men to overturn His plan, or to delay for a moment its accomplishment. Whatever He permits, He keeps the reins in His own hand.

He were a foolish or a careless driver that would let fall the reins as a coach was going down a steep descent — not such a one is God. Whatever perils may surround His Church, it is our exceeding consolation that the reins of government are in the hand of One who orders all things after the counsel of His will, who can bring light out of darkness, and order out of confusion! Yes, He shall make all the calamities of nations, the troubles of His Church, and the doings of His fiercest enemies pay their tribute unto Him.

For the day hastens on apace when the Savior shall come back and take His kingdom for Himself. True it is that now we lift up our eyes to Him, dwelling in the heavens at the Father's right hand — but it shall not be always thus. "You men of Galilee," said the angel, "Why stand you gazing up into Heaven? This same Jesus which is taken up from you into Heaven, shall so come in like manner as you have seen Him go into Heaven." Jesus shall return in glory, and then shall the evils that beset us flee away forever. All the false glare of the present scene shall fade away. All the attractions of a superstitious and sensuous worship shall be seen to be but vanity. All that has been of faith and love, all that has been the fruit of the Spirit of God, shall abide; and all who have been faithful to the Master shall receive an open reward.

It must have been no small source of gratification to the Highland servants of our Queen, who had been faithful and trusty in their service, when their Sovereign mentioned their names in a work read by so many of her subjects. Just so, what will be the deep, heartfelt gladness of those who shall hear from the lips of One exalted far above an earthly throne, their names confessed and approved by Him, in the presence of His Father and the holy angels!

No more shall they then have need to lift up their eyes to the heavens, for they shall dwell there in the mansions of the Father's house. And He to whom when on earth they so often turned, shall dwell among them, and shall be their everlasting Portion!

The Door Open — and the Door Shut!

"But while they were on their way to buy the oil, the bridegroom arrived. The virgins who were ready went in with him to the wedding banquet. And the door was shut!" Matthew 25:10

"The door was shut!" What words are these! How solemnly do they fall upon the ear! They remind us of the passing death-bell. They sound as the death knell of precious souls. Yet are they not also words of mercy, of tender pity, of compassionate love? Were they not the words of Him who was Love Incarnate — the God of love clothed in our flesh? And why did Christ speak them? What feeling prompted their utterance? Was it not love — love to the guilty, love to those as yet far from His kingdom? It was as if He would say, "The door is open now, but it is only for a while before it is closed, and forever, enter in and be saved."

The door was not shut then, to those who heard Christ speak these words. It is not shut now, to us who read them. Side by side with them may be placed the declaration made to the Church of Philadelphia: "These things says He who is holy, He who is true, He who has the key of David, He who opens, and no man shuts; and shuts, and no man opens. I know Your works: behold I have set before you an open door, and no man can shut it." (Rev. 3:7, 8.)

The door open. This is now our blessed privilege. Past years have fled, but the hand of Our God has been over us for good, guarding us in safety through their many dangers. His watchful eye has ever been upon His children, and His everlasting arm beneath them. His patience, His forbearance and long-suffering, have as yet been exercised toward the rebellious: "It is of the Lord's mercies that we are not consumed, because His compassions fail not." (Lam. 3:22.)

The door shut. Even so is it with many who were with us in years past. So will it be with many others before a few months or years more shall have passed away. So will it be with all, for weal or for woe, when the Lord appears as the Judge of the living and the dead.

Look on both sides. May the Spirit of God write upon our inmost souls the twofold message.

I. The Door OPEN.

(1) The door is open to the HOUSE OF GOD. Here, in our Christian land, churches are multiplied, the means of grace increased, special services frequently held, the invitation given continually: "Come and let us go up to the house of the Lord." The door is open — why not enter in? Why are there so many who trample upon Christian ordinances? It was said by one of old, "A day in Your courts is better than a thousand. I had rather be a doorkeeper in the house of my God, than to dwell in the tents of wickedness." (Psalm 84.10.)

Here is the meeting-place of God's dear children, high and low, rich and poor, one with another. Here the voice of united prayer arises as a cloud of incense before the throne. Here we begin to lisp the new song of praise to our God, and to the Lamb. Here we hearken to the voice of apostles, prophets, martyrs — yes, to the voice of the Son of God Himself. Here the promise is fulfilled, "Where two or three are gathered together in My name, there am I in the midst of them." Here, in answer to believing prayer, the Spirit is poured forth — a living power rests upon Christ's ambassador — dead souls are quickened to new life — the soul searching after God, finds rest in Christ — the believer, sore and hindered through temptation, is strengthened and comforted on his way to Zion.

Who can number the blessings that may be found in the regular, devout attendance at the house of God?

Oh, do not shut against yourself, by refusing, or neglecting, to enter into this open door! A very wicked woman, in middle life, was warned by the writer not to neglect the means of grace. "I dare say I may come some day," was the reply. The answer was made to her: "Life is uncertain; our time may not be God's time." It proved but too true in her case. Within a few weeks she was carried as a corpse into that church which she refused to enter when alive. The opportunity was past — the door was shut!

(2) The door is open to an eternal FRIENDSHIP WITH GOD. Oh, what a high and lofty privilege is this! Who can tell the bliss of being on peaceful terms of friendship with the Most High God? In the friendship of God, what safe guardianship, what sure provision, what wise direction, what loving chastisement, what peace, such as the world gives not! If God is one with me — if He is on my side — if He is indeed my Friend, my reconciled Father — why need I fear? What harm can ever reach me? The great enemy shall not prevail against my soul, fears and sorrows shall not overwhelm me, death shall not terrify me. Oh, what quiet rest of spirit is there in walking through this troublesome world, having by my side an Almighty, an ever-faithful, an ever-loving Friend!

But can it be — a sinful man in friendship with the thrice holy Jehovah? Yes. "Enoch walked with God." "Abraham was called the friend of God." The call of mercy is still heard: "Peace, peace to him that is afar off, and to him that is near, says the Lord, and I will heal him." God still waits to be gracious. As the widow left her door unlatched, by day and by night, ever longing for the return of her erring child — so is it with our Father in Heaven. He longs for the return of His wanderers, and is ever ready to welcome them to His bosom. But how can it be? Is not wrath gone out from the Lord? Is it not written, that "the wrath of God is revealed from Heaven against all unrighteousness and ungodliness of men"?

How then can God become the Friend of the sinner? Only by virtue of the mediatorial work of Christ. Christ has become our Ransom, our Substitute. Our guilt has been charged to Him, that we, through Him, might be brought near to God.

An illustration will bring this home to us. Years ago a ship was wrecked on the shore of one of the Coral Islands. The sailors were cruelly butchered, and the spoil of the ship appropriated by the Islanders. Eighteen months passed away, and an English man-of-war approaches the Island, to demand reparation for the crime. During those eighteen months, the Word of God, for the first time, has been proclaimed there; and now the Islanders feel grieved and ashamed for their former crimes.

But what is to be done? They cannot undo the past. They cannot deny the crime which they committed. How can they escape the punishment that is due? They hold a council. One of the tribe addresses them: "Tomorrow the great English captain will come on shore: we cannot deny what we have done; we have no compensation that he will accept. Now, my proposition is this: "Who is there of you that is willing to give up himself to save the rest? Who of you is willing to be sold as a slave, to be put in irons on the ship, or to suffer death, as the captain may choose, so that he may spare our island?" The appeal was not in vain. Four brave men stood forward. They offered to give themselves up to save their nation. The captain was satisfied. The proof of their contrition was so evident, that he freely forgave them, and traded with them.

This incident reminds us, in some measure, of the love of Christ. Our lives were justly forfeited. Our iniquities have brought upon us the righteous displeasure of the great God. But Christ stands forth. He offers Himself as our Ransom. He undertakes to suffer all that may be needful to make atonement for our sins, and to honor God's holy law. He dies an accursed death on our behalf. So God freely forgives us. He receives us back into friendship with Himself. Once strangers, enemies, and rebels to God — we are freely reconciled through the death of His Son.

The door is now open: the heart of God is toward us: the great barrier of human guilt is taken out of the way.

Let those who stand without, now enter in. Hearken to the call of Christ: "I am the door: by Me if any man enter in, he shall be saved, and shall go in and out, and find pasture." (John 10:9.)

Do you feel in your heart that you are not happy with God? You regard Him rather as One to be feared, than loved. You have nothing of the spirit and mind of a dear child with a beloved parent. You shrink from His presence, rather than delight in it. But why should this continue?

Why should there be this estrangement between you and your merciful Creator? Only be willing to yield up the sin which grieves Him; only acknowledge, with genuine contrition, that you have gone astray, like a lost sheep; only come back with filial confidence through the reconciling blood.

Then believe in your Father's love. Put far away every gloomy suspicion that God may possibly reject you. Rejoice in that blessed exchange which is made whenever the soul relies for acceptance only on Jesus and His salvation. You make over to Him your sins; He makes over to you His glorious righteousness. Oh, what eternal glory does this exchange bring to the Son of God! What eternal gladness and peace to the heart of the sinner!

Then is God evermore your Father and your Friend. Then may you sing along your pilgrimage your cheerful hymn of praise and hope: "Being justified by faith, we have peace with God through our Lord Jesus Christ: by whom also we have access by faith into this grace wherein we stand, and rejoice in hope of the glory of God." (Romans 5.1, 2.)

(3) The door is open to the THRONE OF GRACE. Where is the meeting-place between God and His children? Not on a throne of solemn majesty, not on the high throne of universal dominion, not on a throne of strict judgment — but on a throne of grace: "Let us therefore" — that is, having a great and merciful High Priest, "come boldly unto the throne of grace, that we may obtain mercy, and find grace to help in time of need."

Well may the assurance of such a means of access embolden us with confidence to draw near!

Imagine for a moment, that on a set day in each year, our beloved Queen were to take her seat upon her throne. She has caused it to be proclaimed far and wide, that on such a day she will be ready to grant all the petitions that may be made to her. What crowds would flock around her! How many would anticipate the hour when they might hope to obtain some long-sought blessing!

Now this sets before us a great reality. What would be impossible in any earthly sovereign, is actually the case with the great and glorious King who reigns in Heaven! His throne of grace is open to the poor and the wretched, to those who feel burdened with ten thousand sins, and troubled by ten thousand needs and sorrows. It is open, not once a year, but every day, every hour, every moment! It is open for the heinous sinner who comes weighed down by the remembrance of a life's transgressions. It is open for the child of God, who comes again and again for the supply of grace which he needs!

The way to this throne is all paved with golden promises. Take but one or two: "Open your mouth wide, and I will fill it." (Psalm 81:10) "It shall come to pass, that before they call, I will answer; and while they are yet speaking, I will hear." (Isaiah 64:24.) Over that throne, the eye of faith can discern, in letters glittering like the bright stars in Heaven, some such invitations as these:
"Ask, and it shall be given you!
Seek, and you shall find!
Knock, and it shall be opened unto you!"

We have also a merciful and gracious Intercessor. His person as the very and eternal Son of God, His tender sympathy, His all-sufficient merits, His atoning blood —

ever the perfect plea of those who trust in it — all assure us
that we never can ask in vain.

Who can describe the preciousness of the gifts to be
obtained at this throne!

Years ago an Indian prince was greatly indebted to
one high in authority for the aid and support he had
rendered to him. History tells us that the prince desired to
give the Englishman some strong proof of the gratitude he
bore towards him. He took him into a vast underground
chamber, where were collected the most costly and
precious jewels — gold and silver almost without limit —
treasures such as before the Englishman had never seen.
When all these had been displayed before him, the Indian
prince bade him to choose whatever he desired — nothing
would be denied him. Whatever he named, he might call
his own.

There is likewise a rich storehouse of costly treasures
which is open to us. Jesus, our great Mediator, holds the
key, and opens it to all who ask in His name, and according
to His Word.

Even the lukewarm Church of Laodicea, does He
invite to partake of these treasures: "I counsel you to buy of
Me gold tried in the fire, that you may be rich; and white
clothing, that you may be clothed, and that the shame of
your nakedness do not appear; and anoint your eyes with
eye-salve, that you may see." (Rev. 3:18.)

Every precious gift is within the reach of the earnest
seeker: "We might beg ourselves rich, if only we would
stretch out our withered hands to the Friend of sinners."

There are gifts for us concerning this present life. Every solid blessing, every earthly comfort that our hearts can desire, shall be granted in answer to our prayers — if only it is consistent with our highest interests.

There are gifts for us concerning the peace and salvation of our souls. Daily pardon for daily sin, more light to understand the Word of Truth, more strength in the Holy Spirit to overcome sin and to walk with God, more joy and peace in believing, the enduring gold of faith and love, the white clothing of a perfect justification in Christ, the eye salve of Divine wisdom in the knowledge of ourselves and of God — all these are in the hand of Jesus for those who call upon Him.

Gifts for ourselves, gifts for those nearest and dearest to us, gifts for the Church of Christ throughout the world — all are bestowed in answer to fervent believing prayer.

Oh, for grace to enter more frequently, more heartily, by the open door to the mercy seat! "I thank God He has given me a praying heart," were the words often on the lips of a dying Christian girl. Surely a praying heart is a gift beyond all price, for it opens wide the door to the reception of every other blessing.

Leaning on the Spirit's aid, endeavor to carry out, in daily practice, the four extensions of prayer given by Paul:

1. Pray under all circumstances. (Philippians 4:6)

2. Pray for all men. (1 Timothy 2:1)

3. Pray in all places. (1 Timothy 2:8)

4. Pray at all times. (1 Thessalonians 5:17)

Then wait for the answer, and be sure it will come. Praying breath is never lost.

> Hannah at Shiloh,
> Jehoshaphat in his chariot,
> Hezekiah on his sick bed,
> Elijah on Mount Carmel,
> Nehemiah in the king's palace,
> Daniel in Babylon,
> Cornelius in Caesarea,
> Paul and Silas in the dungeon —

these, and the whole company of redeemed and sanctified souls, bear witness to the faithfulness of God in hearkening to the prayers of His children.

(4) The door is open for SERVICE in Christ's vineyard. The message comes to one and all: "Son, daughter — go work today in My vineyard." The apostle, writing of the opportunity for Christian effort at Ephesus, declares, "A great and effectual door is opened unto me, and there are many adversaries." Such a great and effectual door is set open before the Church of Christ in our day, and it is true also that the adversaries are many. Great are the efforts of a refined skepticism to uproot the foundations of the Christian faith — denying all that is supernatural — casting aside, as the tradition of a bygone age, such blessed truths as the inspiration of Scripture, and the perfect atonement made for sin in the precious blood of Christ.

Great are the difficulties we must contend with, both in our own sinful hearts and in the world around, if we would faithfully and successfully labor for Christ. Yet in Him is laid up for us all-sufficient grace and strength. First entering in by the open door to the mercy-seat, and thence obtaining from above wisdom and strength — we may enter in at the door of Christ's vineyard, and our work shall not be in vain. Doors of service open around us on every side. There is work for the believer in his own home, to endeavor to gather his own kindred and household into the fold of Christ. There is work in our cities, our towns, our villages, and our retired hamlets, to instruct the ignorant, to convince the gainsayer, to arouse the sinner, to restore the wanderer. There is work in our schools, our workhouses, our jails, our hospitals. There is work among our soldiers and our sailors. There is work in the various mission-fields, now so marvelously opened to us in the providence of God.

Bear in mind that there is no position in life which need hinder us, if only Christ's love is in our hearts, from doing work for Him

"Wherever in the world I am,
In whatsoever estate,
I have a fellowship with hearts
To keep and cultivate,
And a work of lowly love to do
For the Lord on whom I wait."

It may be the faithful pastor, who in public and in private, by the Word of Truth and by a holy life, is ever preaching Christ.

Or the patient teacher, who in the school or the family leads a little flock to the Savior's footstool.

It may be the Christian of ample means, who watches narrowly his own expenditure, that he may cast the more into the Lord's treasury.

Or, on the other hand, the servant of Christ in humble life, who quietly, prayerfully, pursues his lowly path, bearing a marked witness for his Master by his consistent conduct, and here and there speaking a word in season,

"Content to fill a little space,
 If God is glorified."

It may be the traveler who sows beside all waters, dropping by the wayside some word of Christ, or some little printed messenger of peace.

It may be one of the Lord's prisoners — the captive of a sick chamber — who glorifies God by patient submission to His will.

It may be the true sister of mercy, who fills all the house where she dwells with the fragrance of kindness and love, and then goes out into the world's highway by word and deed, to comfort and support the poor and afflicted.

Or the mother, who finds her sphere of work chiefly among her children, training up a godly seed, watching and praying anxiously for their soul's welfare, and walking before them in the narrow path.

Oh, Christian, go work for Christ while you may! By word or by letter, by your cheerful gifts, by your prayers, by your influence with others — in some way or other do good service in Christ's vineyard.

It is a service full of blessing. There is a reward now, in the joy of the service itself. There is a still higher reward hereafter, in souls saved, and in the Master's approval. It is written, "He who waters shall be watered also himself."

(Proverbs 11.25.) "If any man serve Me let him follow Me; and where I am, there shall also my servant be. If any man serve Me — him will my Father honor." (John 12.26.)

> "Make haste, O man, to do
> Whatever must be done;
> You have no time to lose in sloth —
> Your day will soon be gone.
>
> "The seed whose leaf and flower,
> Though poor in human sight,
> Bring forth at last the eternal fruit —
> So sow both day and night."

(5) The door is open to the EVERLASTING KINGDOM. When Jesus had overcome the sharpness of death — He opened the kingdom of Heaven to all believers. None are shut out who seek for admittance now in the name of the great Mediator. The door is open to the least, and to the greatest — to the little child who has learned to lisp the Savior's name, and to the aged believer who falls asleep after long service in the vineyard. The dying thief, who in deep contrition sought mercy in his last hour, and the Apostle of the Gentiles, who spent years in toils and sufferings for Christ — both knocked and were admitted. Here is the final blessing, the perfect enjoyment of fellowship with the Father and the Son, the full answer to every faithful prayer, the full recompense for every toil and gift. Here the voice of the Beloved shall greet us with a joyful welcome: "Well done, good and faithful servant — enter into the joy of your Lord!"

II. The Door SHUT.

The glorious privilege of an open door remains not with us forever. Now the means of grace abound; a voice of tender compassion entreats the sinner to lay down his arms and be at peace with God; repeated invitations allure us to the mercy-seat; doors of usefulness are every day set before us, Heaven's gate stands open. Whoever will, may enter in. But the time is short. With each of us, the sands of life are quickly running out. Friends, neighbors, relations are gone to their long home — and we are treading fast upon their heels. A man spoke once of the means of his conversion to God: "I looked into my wife's grave," he said, "and I thought 'That is the way I too am going.'" Let us speak thus to our hearts: as we look into the graves of those called away, let us remember we must soon follow along the same path.

The coming of the Son of man is also hastening on. How many years may roll round, or how few, before that great crisis arrives — who can foretell? At the longest we can scarcely imagine it to be very far distant. Then at least, with all mankind, will the day of grace be past — the door will be shut.

How was it in the days of Noah? They ate, they drank, they married — the preacher of righteousness sounded in vain a loud call to repentance, the hundred and twenty years of God's patient longsuffering passed by, the family of the patriarch are safely gathered within the enclosure of the prepared refuge; then "the Lord shut him in" — "the door was shut."

So shall it be when the Lord's chosen ones have been gathered within the true ark: when every one of His elect, by the mighty power of the Spirit, have found eternal safety in Christ. Then the once despised Nazarene shall appear in His glory, and the door will be shut. Hearken to Christ's own words in the parable of the ten virgins: "At midnight there was a cry made, Behold the Bridegroom comes; go out to meet Him." The foolish virgins discover too late how unprepared they are. Their lamps are gone out, and they have no oil in the vessel. They go to buy, if perchance even now they may be in time; but what happens?

"But while they were on their way to buy the oil, the bridegroom arrived. The virgins who were ready went in with him to the wedding banquet. And the door was shut. Later the others also came. 'Sir! Sir!' they said. 'Open the door for us!' But he replied, 'I tell you the truth, I don't know you.' Therefore keep watch, because you do not know the day or the hour!" Matthew 25:10-13

"The door was shut." Here again do we see mercy and judgment mingled together. What a thought of exceeding consolation is suggested by the shut door! Look within that shut door. Oh, what joy unspeakable, what security, what fellowship with the Father and the Son! "Blessed are those who are called to the marriage supper of the Lamb." The shut door has forever excluded every possible evil. There shall be . . .
no more temptation,
no more wanderings from God,
no more racking pains,
no more heart-aches,
no more sighing and sadness because of iniquity around,
no more distressing anxieties or bitter disappointments,
no more partings,

no more death!

"God will wipe every tear from their eyes. There will
be no more death or mourning or crying or pain, for the old
order of things has passed away." Revelation 21:4

Within that shut door, is found every member of the
household of faith. The whole family of God, once
separated by a thousand barriers of earth, by seas and
continents, by diversity of opinion, by rank and position in
life — are now gathered together within the many
mansions of the Father's house.

Abel the first martyr,
Enoch who for three hundred years and more walked
with God,
Abraham the father of the faithful,
Moses the lawgiver of Israel,
the three righteous ones, Noah, Daniel, and Job,
David the man after God's own heart,
the glorious company of the apostles,
the goodly fellowship of the prophets,
the noble army of martyrs and missionaries,
the pastor and his flock,
the diligent worker,
the patient sufferer,
the busy Marthas and the devout Marys who have both
truly loved the Savior — all shall sit down together in the
kingdom of God.

And Jesus Himself, the chief among ten thousand, is
there in the midst! Who can tell the joy that the immediate
presence of the Redeemer will bring to myriads of happy
spirits? Have you never felt what a ray of sunshine entered
your home when some loving disciple of Christ sat down

and conversed with you of the things of God? What then will it be when the very Sun of Righteousness — He who is the Fountain-head of all those excellencies which shine forth in His people — shall Himself be visibly present with you?

Here, too, in "the shut door," have we the assurance of the abiding, unchangeable security of the redeemed. "The shut door" forever forbids the possibility that any shall fall away, as the angels once fell from their high estate. It is written, "Him that overcomes, I will make a pillar in the temple of my God, and he shall go no more out." (Rev. 3:12.) With saints and angels — yes, with the Lamb Himself — shall the saved be eternally shut in.

But look for a moment on the OUTER side of the shut door: "Outside are the dogs, those who practice magic arts, the sexually immoral, the murderers, the idolaters and everyone who loves and practices falsehood!" Revelation 22:15

What a strangely mingled company are gathered together there! The unjust — and the unholy! The criminal whose course on earth was cut short by the hand of the executioner — and the man who blameless before his fellow-man, had yet trampled on the holy Law of God! The open despiser of Christ and His people — and the clever hypocrite who deceived all but God! The wicked, the profane, the profligate, the dishonest — side by side with the respectable worldling, the amiable trifler, the slave of fashion, the lover of pleasure, the secret worshiper of Mammon! The kind neighbor who knew not and loved not Christ, nor trusted in His salvation. Oh, how fearful to many of the unsaved will be that mingling together, in one awful company, of those who have never been one with

Christ; and who, with many differences, have alike never experienced the regenerating power of the Spirit of God!

And where shall their lot be cast? Outside the marriage feast — and within the prison house of God's everlasting wrath! Within that dark abode of wretchedness and woe and despair, where no ray of hope can ever come! Where the lips that cannot lie have told us, that there "the worm never dies, and the fire is never quenched."

The door was shut — never to be re-opened. Many are asking, "Shall there not be an end? Shall the punishment of the sinner indeed be for evermore? When years, centuries, and ages have rolled by, may we not hope that the mercy of God may discover some way of escape, so that all at length may find repose in the bosom of the great Parent?" We would hope it — but we may not — we dare not! That Word, upon which hangs our every hope, has declared it otherwise. He has said, "The door was shut!" He has told us of the cry of those unprepared: "Lord, Lord, open to us." But the shut door cannot be re-opened. The answer is decisive: "Truly I say unto you, I know you not." In the very same sentence has He proclaimed the bliss of those on the right hand, and the doom of those on the left, to be of equal duration, and that forever: "These shall go away into everlasting punishment — but the righteous unto everlasting life!" (Matthew 25.46.)

"The door was shut." "What door?" asks one. "That door now open to those who come from the east and the west, the north and the south — that door which says, "Him that comes unto Me, I will never cast out." Behold how now that door is open — which shall then be closed evermore. Murderers come, and are admitted. Profligate sinners come, and they are received. The wicked, the

sexually immoral, the idolaters, the adulterers, the
homosexual offenders, the thieves, the drunkards come —
and the open door does not deny itself to them! For Christ
Himself is the door — infinite to pardon, almighty to save.

What says Christ now? "I am the door! By Me if any
man enter in he shall be saved." What says He then? 'The
door is shut.' No one's penitence, no one's prayers, no one's
groanings shall any more be admitted. The door is shut
which received . . .
Aaron after idolatry,
David after adultery,
Manasseh after murder,
Peter after his three-fold denial!

"Once the owner of the house gets up and shuts the
door, you will stand outside knocking and pleading, 'Sir,
open the door for us.' But he will answer, 'I don't know you
or where you come from.' Then you will say, 'We ate and
drank with you, and you taught in our streets.' But he will
reply, 'I don't know you or where you come from. Away
from me, all you evildoers!' There will be weeping there,
and gnashing of teeth, when you see Abraham, Isaac and
Jacob and all the prophets in the kingdom of God — but
you yourselves thrown out!" Luke 13:25-28

It is the voice of a merciful Redeemer that calls forth
His people to work in His vineyard. When in Egypt the
taskmasters bade the Israelites go forth to their hard toil, it
was but in hopeless despair that they betook themselves to
their work. But it is the voice of love which we hear. He
who says, "Son, be of good cheer, your sins be forgiven,"
says also to each of His forgiven ones, "Son, go work today
in my vineyard."

Hence is it as a privilege, rather than as a duty, we hear and obey the call. Let us picture to ourselves the prodigal son in the parable, who had been so lovingly welcomed home. Let us imagine, on the day following his return, his father pointing out to him some needful work in the field, and desiring him to perform it. With what gladsome heart, with what willing feet, would he have fulfilled his father's bidding! He would not have said, "I will go, sir," while yet he went not. Neither would he have refused, even for a time, the command given to him. Rather would he with the utmost alacrity at once have accepted, and immediately have gone forth to accomplish the work.

In such a spirit let us hear God's message to us. Forgetting the things which are behind — let us reach forth unto those which are before. Let us heartily and cheerfully labor in the Lord's vineyard.

The Master has given to every man his work. The time for doing it is but short. If it is left undone, how shall we meet the Master at His appearing, and give account of the talents He has committed to us?

The subject is a very practical one, and of immense importance to Christ's Church, and the welfare of His people. Sloth, idleness, indifference to the cause of truth and the good of others — is a canker, a rust that greatly injures the gold and silver vessels of the Lord's house. While active, laborious, self-denying work for Christ brings its reward, even now, in an increased measure of spiritual life.

How may Christian people labor happily, effectively, successfully in the Lord's vineyard? The utmost I can hope to do is to offer a few suggestions in answer to this inquiry, which by God's grace may afford some direction to those who are seeking it.

1. Christ's work for us, and not our work for Him — must be the sole ground of all our hope and confidence. Not the labor of our hands, not our gifts or prayers or tears, not our zeal or self-denial — but Christ's great work of redemption is the sure resting-place for the soul of each sinful child of Adam. For what could be our merit? What do we have, that we have not received? What are we but stewards — whether of life, ability, talents, wealth, influence, or anything else that we can employ for God. Could we do all commanded to us, as we never can — yet what are we then but unprofitable servants. What reparation can we make for the neglects and misdeeds of days and years gone by? How can we undo the evil already wrought? Shall I tell those who have been wasting their substance, and forgetting the claims of their Savior and their God, that by double diligence in the future they may atone for the past, and weave for themselves a garment that will shield them from the divine justice which they have provoked? Nay, what were this but to set at naught the very purpose of the Redeemer's death?

If you ask, "By what work may former sin be blotted out, and my conscience be clear from guilt?" I would answer plainly and simply, "The work completed long ago, when Jesus died and rose again. That work is perfect and all-sufficient, and you cannot add to it.

He bore your sin;
He endured your penalty;
He paid your ransom;
He wrought out for you a glorious righteousness — in this alone you must stand. To know and realize this will be

your joy and strength. Strongly lean on the promise of life through Christ crucified; firmly believe that the penitent sinner, taking hold of Christ's blood, will never be cast away. With all humility, trusting thus in the death and obedience of your Surety, you will have a freeness of heart, and a motive for labor, which nothing else can possibly supply.

2. Christ's Spirit working in us is our great qualification in working for Christ.

In the second chapter of the Epistle to the Ephesians, the Apostle Paul very clearly sets forth the position which good works occupy in a Christian's life. He bids the Ephesian Church remember that they are saved by grace through faith. This salvation is bestowed gratuitously. It is not the purchase of their doings, but the gift of God to be received by the hand of faith: "not of works, lest any man should boast."

But is there no place left for works? Is it possible to be saved without such? Nay, for it is the very object for which men are created anew in Christ Jesus: it is the very path which God has marked out for men to tread. It is not the instrument of salvation, but the end of it. It is not the way to obtain life, but the sure result wherever God works within the soul: "We are His workmanship, created in Christ Jesus unto good works, which God has before ordained that we should walk in them."

As the potter takes the clay and molds it according to his will to form a vessel for himself, so does God by His own Spirit take hold of a sinful child of Adam. He . . .
reveals to him sin in its true character,

brings home to him in power the knowledge of His own marvelous love,

manifests to him the exceeding great and precious promises of the Word,

opens out before him the glorious prospect of the everlasting kingdom.

And thus God creates within him new desires, new dispositions, filial confidence, grateful love, fervent zeal and humble charity — the marks of His own image formed within the soul.

Hence the Spirit's presence must be our chief qualification in Christ's work. For whatever we do, our Father's eye rests not on the outward deed, but on the spirit in which it is performed, and on the motive that prompts it. With a bright light placed before the eye, the physician can discern, by means of the ophthalmoscope, that which is amiss on the innermost retina. Just so, does our God search out the most secret feelings that lurk within the breast. And only as He sees our works done out of true love to Him, does He accept them at our hands. Moreover, it is the Spirit who stirs up and quickens the heart to self-denying effort, who suggests plans of usefulness, and gives the needful wisdom and grace to carry them out. From first to last He is the great Worker, and we work in Him and with Him and for Him.

As in machinery there is a central force which moves all the various wheels and rods, and then each in its place performs its proper part, even so does the grace of Christ's Spirit inspire and move Christian hearts, working in us both to will and to do after God's good pleasure.

Be this, Christian, your strength and your dependence. Lean on the Spirit's aid — cast yourself wholly upon His ready help.

For wisdom and for boldness,
for love to the Master and compassion for the souls,
for perseverance in work already in hand,
or for grace to attempt fresh labors —
do all in the Holy Spirit. "Not by might, nor by power, but by my Spirit, says the Lord."

3. We must each one be workers:
not idlers,
not talkers,
not merely framers of plans and theories,
not murmurers because others do so little —
but busy, active, diligent workers in the vineyard.

Far too much time is wasted in surmising what we might effect in some other position, or under other circumstances, if we had the means possessed by someone else, or the leisure or influence possessed by another; or perhaps questioning whether it were possible to do some necessary work. Be sure there is some work you can do, and the best way to learn how to do it is to go and try. The practical experience of half an hour will probably do more than weeks of previous consideration. I am not speaking against due forethought in work, for we are told to prepare our work before-hand, and afterwards to build our house. But I do speak against weeks and months being thrown away because persons are hesitating and considering so long that the time for the effort is past. The point I urge is this: you have a work to do, a great work, and you must strive to discover what it is, and then labor hard in the doing of it.

There are nearly five hundred joints, small or great, in the human body. If each joint does not perform its due function, the whole body suffers. Just so is it in the body of Christ. Each member has his place, and if he neglects his work, it will be left undone, to his loss, the dishonor of Christ, and the great injury of His Church.

An earnest Church must be a thoroughly working Church, with all its members animated by one spirit; like the bees in a hive — all busy each in his own department, and all adding to the common stock of devoted labor for Christ, His Church and the world. Over the portals of every church should be inscribed, "Let no man enter here who is not determined to be holy and useful."

4. We must not hold back from the work to which God is calling us, because of our own insufficiency.

Perhaps the reason why Christians so often shrink back from working for Christ, is because they are not content to be simply instruments in God's hand for doing whatever He will by them. They wish to do something themselves, instead of being willing that God should take them and use them in any way that He sees fit. To be an earthen cup, which the owner may fill with water and pass round to the guests and then lay aside on the shelf; or to be a pen which must be first made, then filled with ink, often cut and sharpened, held by the hand, and only employed to write the thoughts of him who holds it — to be willing to be something like this in God's hand may not be very flattering to our pride, but it is the only way in which we can expect to be useful.

It is only thus God will make use of us to give to others the living water, or to write His epistles, and to inscribe His thoughts on the tablet of human hearts. And for our consolation, let us remember that when in felt weakness and insufficiency we go at the Master's bidding to do something in His service, we shall probably reap much blessing on our own souls, while also He prospers the effort we make for Him.

5. We must take a wide view of the field of labor. If only the eye be open to survey it, it stretches out before us in every direction. Nowhere can we turn, but there is a call to work.

There is work for Christ at our own fireside. We have to commend Christ to our own kindred, and to any who may dwell under the same roof with us. We must watch for opportunities of speaking a word in due season — a wise word, a kind word, and at the right moment.

Yet I am persuaded it is here that consistent, holy living counts far more than words. A holy life preaches every hour, and scatters a sweet savor of Christ to influence those we love. If our words for Christ are but few, yet our holy example should give them a meaning and weight that leaves a deep impression. It were well if every hour and every moment we could let others perceive in us something of Christ.

There is a simple Persian fable that may teach us the value of this. A man takes within his hand a piece of scented clay. "You smell very sweetly — what are you?" he asks. "I am only a piece of clay," is the reply; "but I have been near a rose, and the rose has given me its own sweet scent."

Would that we could keep near the Rose of Sharon, and then so live in spirit, in temper, in charity, in self-denial, in gentleness — that others might take knowledge of us that we have been with Christ!

We have work to do in the congregation to which we belong. I know of no more important duty for each Christian than striving to be a real strength in the church where he may worship. Too many, alas, are our weakness and our sorrow. They hear the Word and that is all. In vain do we look to them for hearty worship within God's house, or for ready sympathy and aid in the work of the parish. The various institutions that need willing hands and helpers, are left without the assistance they so urgently require. Let it not be thus with any reader of these pages. Let your pastor know and feel that to the utmost of your ability, you will take your place by his side and strengthen his hand in God's work. Let him feel that he can thoroughly depend upon your influence being exerted for good, and your willingness to fill up a niche where you may be of use. There are funds to be collected, school children to be gathered in and instructed, the sick to be cared for, church functions to be arranged perhaps, and numberless other things which will impede the work of the pastorate, and prevent his being at liberty for spiritual duties — unless you are willing to do your part in assisting him.

We have work to do in the dwellings of the rich and the poor. Never forget that your friends who have large means and live in much comfort, have equal need to know Christ and His salvation — as those that have the least of this world's good. And sometimes they have still more need of a word of faithful and friendly counsel, because their position stands in the way of the plain-speaking they require. Much may be done in such a case, though it demands special wisdom. By a letter or by a book lent or given, you may often make some impression. And as death and sickness and trial visit the homes of all alike — there will occur the opportunity you desire of speaking personally a word in season.

A clergyman more than once is refused admittance to the house of an officer who had lately lost a beloved child. Still he repeats the call, and finds an open door for speaking to him of Him who alone can give true consolation. By the grace of God the message is made of lasting benefit, and in the end great spiritual blessings result, both to the family and the parish of him who so faithfully witnessed for Christ.

And is there not a crying need for fresh work to be done among our working population? In any parish, town or country, in any part of the land, is there not enough to awaken our deepest compassion, as we behold such numbers living without the least regard to His word? In spite of all past efforts, very small is the proportion of those who ever enter the walls of God's house, while intemperance and kindred evils abound and increase.

What can be done? Could not more work be done by means of special services for working people in churches or in school-rooms? Could there not be found visitors who would take an interest in a few families — say six or eight — and search out thoroughly that which in each case is the hindrance, and strive by personal kindness and influence to lift some at least of these a step higher? Might there not be more general efforts to save the young, and perseveringly to sow the good seed in their hearts, that in spite of all hindrances, might in many cases bring a harvest of blessing? These little ones have hitherto known nothing but either foolish indulgence or harsh words and hasty blows — who shall say what might be effected by the omnipotence of kindness?

No doubt great difficulties stand in the way, yet by earnest zeal and faith in God's power, the mountain might be leveled, and trophies won for Christ.

There is work to be done in resisting to the very utmost of our power the perilous errors which on all sides beset us. The law of love never bids us shut our eyes, or close our lips when false teaching is rife. Nay, to oppose it is the truest charity. For if truth is the soul's food, and ignorance is the soul's starvation — it is equally true that error in things essential to salvation, is the soul's poison. Hence, where is the charity of leaving men to drink in those unscriptural views which are so widely taught, without pointing out the danger to which they are exposed?

The doctrine of the Presence of Christ in the sacramental elements, and a sacrificial offering, leading on to an adoration which we fear in God's sight is nothing better than worshiping an idol within His temple — hymns sung to Mary, leading on most surely to all the creature-worship of the Romish Church — the authority of Holy Scripture either set at nothing and rejected openly, or with more specious subtlety its power to control the conscience undermined — such evils as these demand the perpetual vigilance of all faithful men, lest in judgment, God permits our light to go out and the candlestick be removed from the midst of us.

There is work to be done for the lands far off from us. The wild wastes of heathendom still need to be reclaimed. But a fringe of light at best, or a little ray of Gospel truth illumines vast Islands and Continents. Think of Asia. Out of some eight hundred million, as they have been computed, at the utmost there are but ten million who bear the name of Christ; leaving seventy million as followers of the false prophet, and more than seven hundred million as pagan idolaters.

"But they are far away, and I have work nearer home." True: but let me ask you, if you are an honest man — would you refuse to pay a debt because the one to whom it was due lived on the other side of the globe? Would it not as much be your duty faithfully to pay it, as if he lived within a few doors of your own home? And has not God laid it as a debt on all who have received His Gospel, to send the knowledge of it to the uttermost parts of the earth?

Oh, think of the heathen in Africa, in China, in India and elsewhere; they have sins offtimes troubling the conscience, as you have; they have their cares and heart-rending sorrows, they have death to face and a judgment seat before which they must appear, but they know not that which God has taught you; they know not of the all-cleansing fountain, and the all-sufficient grace and the all-consoling love which support and comfort you. Think of them. Pray for them. Send to them the light that shines into your heart. He who has this world's good — and still more, he who has that which is good for both worlds — and sees his brother have need, and shuts up his affections of compassion from him, how dwells the love of God in him?

In laboring in any of these portions of Christ's vineyard, joyfully accept the least and humblest task which the Master may assign to you. Wait not for great opportunities, but be on the look-out perpetually to do some little where you may. It is not lost labor . . .

to wipe away the tear of a child,
to carry a burden for a weary one,
to remove a stray weed,
to drop in a single grain of good seed,
to strengthen some tendril of the true vine which may
have been loosened by some wind of temptation,
to be a hewer of wood or a drawer of water,
to shine like a glow-worm if not like a star,
to remove a stone which might make a little one to
stumble,
to give a cup of cold water to one that is thirsty,
or by a kind word to comfort a cheerless heart.

Eliot, the apostle to the Indians, was found on his
death-bed instructing a little child to read, and when asked
why he would not now be content to rest, he said that he
desired God would make him useful, and though he had no
longer strength to preach, he had strength to teach a child,
and therefore he gladly did it. "Mind not high things — but
condescend to men of low estate."

Together with this let there be a holy ingenuity in
discovering means of doing good. What you cannot effect
in one way, see if you cannot in another. It may be that for
six days your necessary business prevents your doing much
direct work in Christ's vineyard, but can you not give an
hour or two on Sunday? You may feel great difficulty in
speaking to others, but can you not write a letter that might
be useful to a friend or relation, or might you not scatter
hither and there Christian publications, or carefully selected
tracts, or even at times a book that might do real good?
There are Christian men who give each Christmas, a large
number of very valuable works to their workmen and
others, and it might bring much blessing if many more
followed their example.

I throw out these suggestions for your consideration. Let the love of Christ constrain you, and then in some way, and in the best way, you will do His work.

Then let there be quiet, steady perseverance in all you undertake. Let not your zeal be damped by difficulties or apparent failure at first. Never turn back. Never give up. Some seed is long under-ground and the gardener has to exercise long patience before the precious harvest is gathered in. "He who believes, shall not make haste." "Be not weary in well doing, for in due season we shall reap if we faint not."

To crown all, let your work be carried on in a spirit of expectant, believing prayer.

There may be much toil in the garden — seed may be sown, the soil broken up, weeds removed, and much beside. But if there be no life-giving showers and no genial sunshine, what will be the profit? And what will be the result of any work we may attempt for Christ, unless in answer to the prayers of His servants He sends down the rain of His grace, the dews of His Spirit, and the warm, cheering beams of His love? Whatever be left undone, let the work of prayer never be neglected.

For our congregations at home,
for those gathered from among the heathen abroad,
for the children and servants in the family,
for the young collected together in our National and Sunday schools,
for the Spirit of God to rest on those in high positions in our land,
for the same Spirit to awaken the masses who are living without God and without hope

— for all this let us fervently and unceasingly supplicate Him who is the Author and Giver of all good, and who delights in the prayers of His believing people.

It may be well for Christ's workers to call to mind the sure consolation which He affords them in His service.

On all sides there is much to depress and discourage. Our own insufficiency, the little fruit we may have seen from that which we have already attempted, the threatening aspect of the future, and the exceeding uncertainty as to the course which events may take both in the Church, in our country and in the world; these things may well tempt us to look on the darker side — yet there is a bright light in the clouds if only we have an eye to see it.

Is it not our exceeding consolation in all work for Christ — that He Himself takes a far deeper interest in its success than we can? It is His work, not ours; and therefore we may leave results confidently in His hands. We may also be well assured that while we act at His bidding, and in reliance upon His aid — He will stand by His servants and afford them a cheering sense of His tender sympathy.

We are told that two parallel nerves pass from each part of the body to the head: by one, the head perceives that which affects the particular member — by the other the head directs the action of that member. Just so, let the Christian remember that in our Exalted Head, Christ Jesus, there is both a similar sympathy and a similar power of direction. He feels for the very least of His people. That which touches them, touches Him — yes, touches, as it were, the apple of His eye. You may be tempted, or opposed and hindered, or by infirmity prevented from doing the work you would otherwise love to do. Yet Jesus understands it all — He accepts the will for the deed. He reckons as faithful service your feeble efforts to do something for His name, yes, and your patient endurance of pain or sorrow, if such is your appointed lot — is as truly work for Him as the active labor of the young missionary who journeys thousands of miles to preach His Gospel.

Then, too, He grants direction. He guides and disposes those who are at work for Him — ordering their path, opening out, as He will, opportunity for good, and then showing them in what way they may employ the opportunity He presents.

May we not also regard it as a most cheering consideration, amidst all our trials and perplexities from the present condition of Christ's Church, that the Lord will carry out to their full completion His own bright designs, and manifest by and by, how surely all His counsels are wisdom and truth and faithfulness.

Never shall I forget an evening spent on the Riffelberg, in the southern part of Switzerland. The rolling masses of dark cloud came up from beneath, and hid from sight the magnificent peak of the Matterhorn. I felt for the moment as if I had lost a friend. But as I watched to discover if possible any traces of its form, gradually the clouds passed by, its glorious head stood out as if touching the sky above, the outline of the right side became visible, and at length the whole prospect was clear, and the grand old mountain was seen if possible more beautiful than before, for the clouds which for a time had concealed it from view.

Even thus, I thought, shall it be with the truth and faithfulness of our God. The unbelief, the doubt, the multiplied errors of the present day — whence come they? Is it not from beneath — from the ignorance and infirmity of man, and the cunning devices of our subtle adversary?

And though they seem to obscure for a short season the bright and blessed hopes which are the heritage of Christ's Church, though they bring darkness and sorrow of heart, and greatly distress the minds of God's people — yet by and by they shall pass away. "Our God is the Rock; His work is perfect, for all His ways are judgment. A God of truth and without iniquity, just and right is He."

The trials of the present shall prepare the way for the coming of the Son of Man. When darkest falls the night, when most gloomy is the horizon — He will come, and all shall be changed. Then shall it be seen that more firm and stable than that mountain peak, is His fidelity to His Word and people. And more glorious shall be the kingdom which He shall introduce for all that has before hindered and opposed its progress.

Let us therefore learn "to labor and to wait." Let us be steadfast, immovable, always abounding in the work of the Lord, knowing that our labor shall not be in vain in the Lord. Let our prayer arise perpetually, that He whom we desire to serve would manifest His power and grace in us and by us. "Let Your work appear unto Your servants, and Your glory unto their children. And let the beauty of the Lord our God be upon us, and establish You the work of our hands upon us — yes, the work of our hands establish it."

Strength for the Strengthless

It is a peculiar excellence of the Gospel of Christ, that it describes man exactly as he is, and brings near to him, exactly as it finds him, the gift of a free and complete salvation.

Imagine a man fallen into a deep pit. It were in vain to tell him that if he had taken heed to his steps, he would never have fallen therein. It were in vain to warn him against falling again, if he once escapes alive. It were equally in vain to promise him that if he would endeavor by his own efforts to climb its precipitous sides, you would assist him as he neared the top. But it would not be in vain if you let down a ladder or a strong rope reaching to the very spot where he was, and then bade him avail himself of the means provided for his rescue.

It was most suitable help that Ebed-melech the Ethiopian, and the thirty men with him, afforded to Jeremiah, when they let down into the cistern where he was sinking in the mire, the cords with which they drew him out, and thus preserved his life. (Jeremiah 38)

Let us apply the illustration to our own condition. Man has fallen — deeply, terribly. He has fallen . . .
from holiness — to sin,
from fellowship with God — to a state of alienation and enmity,
from a home in paradise — to the peril of being cast forever into the bottomless pit.

And whence can our help come? There are systems that can give excellent rules of moral conduct, that can promote a partial reformation of life and manners, that can do something for those who might be able first to raise themselves; but all this is of little avail to those who, like ourselves, are by nature altogether unholy and condemned. This is but to give counsel to the man in the pit, or at least to promise him aid which is very insufficient.

But Christ is mighty to help and deliver. Who can tell the length of His saving arm? It reaches the very spot where we are. He not merely counsels us to walk in the right way, or promises to assist those who first help themselves — but He comes near with grace and help to the sinner at the time of his utmost misery and need. He calls not the righteous, but sinners to repentance. He receives sinners, even the chief; forgiving all their iniquities, and healing all their infirmities. He cries to the children of men, "O Israel, you have destroyed yourself, but in Me is your help."

He tells them that they are lost, guilty, and polluted; blind, wretched, poor, and naked; helpless and undone, without strength to rise above the evil; yes, captives of the prince of darkness, and dead in trespasses and sins! And then He offers to raise them from this condition to glory, honor and immortality! He bids them yield themselves up into His hand, to be saved and sanctified by Him; and He undertakes to do the whole work from first to last. He will give all they need:
eye-salve for the recovering of sight,
white clothing for their nakedness,
the finest gold for their poverty,
pardon for all their guilt,
cleansing for all their pollution,
freedom for bondage, and
life spiritual and eternal to those dead in sin.

Hence it is our part in all sincerity to welcome this great salvation, to give full credit to the word of promise and invitation, not to put it aside because of personal demerit, failure, inability, or the like — but on all these accounts the more gladly to accept it; to rest upon it as most sure and stable, and to expect its fulfillment in due season. This is to enter in by the door that God has opened, and to take hold of the covenant which He has made with us in Christ.

Among the precious benefits of the covenant of grace, there is nothing that more demands our thankfulness than the strength promised to the strengthless. "As your days — so shall your strength be." "The God of Israel is He who gives strength and power to His people." "I will strengthen them in the Lord, and they shall walk up and down in His name, says the Lord."

In the fortieth chapter of the Prophet Isaiah, we have a very gracious promise of strength to the feeble and the fearful, and a promise, too, peculiarly applicable to the commencement of a new year. "Do you not know? Have you not heard? The LORD is the everlasting God, the Creator of the ends of the earth. He will not grow tired or weary, and his understanding no one can fathom. He gives strength to the weary and increases the power of the weak. Even youths grow tired and weary, and young men stumble and fall; but those who hope in the LORD will renew their strength. They will soar on wings like eagles; they will run and not grow weary, they will walk and not be faint." Isaiah 40:28-31

The utter insufficiency of man stands out very prominently in this passage. A man, through loss of blood, or for some other cause, is ready to faint; who can be weaker than he is at that moment? Yet to such a one is the promise made: "He gives power to the faint." It is not those who have a fair amount of strength for ordinary circumstances — it is not for those who boast a little strength which needs to be supplemented, but it is "to those who have no might, He increases strength."

Never forget that man has no inherent strength whatever. "When we were yet without strength, Christ died for the ungodly." "We have no power of ourselves to help ourselves." There is nothing in man's nature to prevent a lapse into the grossest iniquities. A rod will stand so long as your hand is upon it; but remove the hand, and it falls in a moment. Adam, created in holiness, yet fell when left to himself. Hezekiah, when God left him to try him, yielded to the very first temptation. Peter, glorying in his superior faithfulness and zeal, yet brings dishonor upon the Master, and denies Him with oaths and curses.

"Fear not, worm, Jacob." Isaiah 41:14

A very striking emblem of the feebleness of man, is given by the Prophet Isaiah. He is likened to a worm that creeps on the ground. The idea is very suggestive.

It reminds us that man is defiled. "How then can a man be righteous before God? How can one born of woman be pure? If even the moon is not bright and the stars are not pure in his eyes — how much less man, who is but a worm!" Job 25:4-6

It reminds us that man is earth-bound. His soul cleaves to the dust. His treasure and his heart is below. I have heard of one in India who found a large clod of earth in a field, and who took it home, saying that it would be his God; and who from that day to his old age, spent his time and money in adorning a temple where he worshiped it. That man stood not alone in his folly. Until the heart is quickened by divine grace, every man makes an idol of a lump of clay.

It may be in the shape of gold,
it may be earthly comforts,
it may be a child,
it may be self.
Whatever it is, it is of the earth, earthy.

The emblem reminds us that man is akin to dust. "He says to corruption, You are my father; to the worm, You are my mother and my sister." The sentence abides unrepealed: "Dust you are, and unto dust shall you return." "The dust shall return to the earth as it was, and the spirit shall return to God who gave it."

And what so feeble as the worm? What power has it of defense or attack? What power has it to resist one who would trample upon it? And where is man's strength? Frail children of dust, and feeble as frail — how can we resist or overcome a single foe?

Very wholesome may be the remembrance of this. Strange is it that man should glory in anything that he possesses. What has he to glory in, that he has not first received? What has he who belongs to earth, from which he must not soon part? O that we might learn deeper humility! O that we might cast away those inner reliances, those inner confidences in our own powers that keep us from leaning all our weight on an Almighty arm, that keep us from looking out of self to Him who is the Lord of all power and might!

Here is the reason that many sink lower and lower, from one depth of iniquity to another, into hopeless miseries and sorrows, into divers temptations, at length, it may be, into utter despair, into irretrievable ruin, and finally into the deep ocean of God's wrath and fiery indignation! "The youths shall faint and be weary, and the young men shall utterly fall." Such live without prayer, without God, without any dependence on the only strength that can uphold them, for they trust in human resources; they are secretly propped up by an idea of something in self that can support — so they fall at length, and fall to rise no more.

> Man's wisdom is to seek
> His strength in God alone;
> For e'en an angel would be weak,
> Who trusted in his own.

And now let us mark how the Almighty Jehovah links Himself to His weak and faltering creature — links His unfailing strength to our feebleness — takes this worm into His hand, as it were, so that in His might we conquer and triumph. He is . . .

the God of all comfort, (Isaiah 40:1)

the God who freely pardons iniquity (verse 2);

the God who tenderly cares for His flock (verse 11);

the God in whose sight all nations are as nothing (verse 15);

the God who creates all the host of Heaven, and calls them by their names by the greatness of His might, because He is strong in power (verse 26);

He is the everlasting God, the Creator of the ends of the earth, who faints not, neither is weary;

He is the God of unerring wisdom, of whose understanding there is no searching. (Verse 28.)

And He brings all this unfailing, everlasting grace, wisdom, and might, to support . . .

those who are cast down,

those who have neither wisdom nor strength,

those who are ready to stumble, and unable to resist a single foe, or advance a single step.

He says, "I am near you, yes, I am with you, to hold you by your right hand. I will strengthen you; yes, I will help you; yes, I will uphold you. I will give you power, I will increase your strength, I will make you stronger than all your foes, so that you shall rejoice in the Lord, and glory in the Holy One of Israel."

It is important to remember that this grace and strength is laid up in Christ, and imparted to us by the Holy Spirit. "'I have laid help upon one that is mighty." "Be strong in the grace which is in Christ Jesus." Through Christ alone, does the Father send help from above. His death has purchased it. His intercession ensures it. He beholds His people in all their straits and dangers, and sends down each moment the strength they need — and this is actually imparted by the agency of the Holy Spirit. Believers are strengthened "with might by the Spirit in the inner man."

He brings near to them the promises of the Word;

He makes the presence of Christ to be a felt reality;

He nerves the soul with patient endurance in suffering;

He strengthens faith, hope, and love —

and so enables them to stand fast in the Lord, and to be more than conquerors through Him.

We must remember also that a single-hearted dependence on the Lord, and continual waiting upon Him in believing prayer, is the never-failing means of securing the aid that is promised. "Those who wait upon the Lord shall renew their strength." Quietly, perseveringly to wait on the Lord with a confiding assurance that none shall seek in vain — this is to be our perpetual resource.

It is said that the creditor in India will sometimes remain at the door of the man who owes him a debt, and will sit there for hours, and refuse to leave until he obtains that which he seeks. Just so, it were well for us to go thus and sit at God's door, with continual importunity waiting upon Him, beseeching Him to endue us mightily with grace and strength. He would not be angry with us, He would not reckon us troublesome suitors — but though all the debt be on our side, He would amply reward our perseverance, and give us — not the crumbs that fall from His table — but the richest provision that His house contains.

And how marvelous is the change that is wrought when a man is endued with strength and power from on high! In himself is he as the worm. In the might of God he is as the eagle soaring upward to the skies, or as the giant rejoicing as a strong man to run a race. Mark how the promise speaks: "those who wait upon the Lord shall renew their strength; they shall mount up with wings as eagles; they shall run and not be weary, and they shall walk and not faint."

Wonderful is the transformation from the worm — to the eagle and the giant! Those once debased, cleaving only to the things of earth — have strength given to rise upward to hold converse with the Father, and to sit in heavenly places with Christ. Those once paralyzed by sin, having neither the power nor the desire to tread the path of life — now . . .

walk unweariedly in the Lord's ways,
run with patience and zeal the heavenly race,
and win the crown of glory and immortality!

We might illustrate by the story of David's conflict
with Goliath, the promise that God makes of imparting
strength to the strengthless. The hosts of Israel and Philistia
are ready to go forth to the battle. Then comes forth the
threatening Philistine with vaunting air and vain-glorious
boastings, to defy the armies of the Lord. "Who will fight
with me?" says he. "Give me a man, that we may fight
together." Is there one bold enough, brave enough to accept
the challenge? Is there one to be found who will venture to
stand up against the champion of the enemy?

Yes, a shepherd lad — one who has just come from
feeding his father's sheep. While all the men of war flee
away in fear and terror — the youthful son of Jesse enters
the lists. His spirit is stirred within him, his courage is
awakened as he hears the dishonor which an uncircumcised
Philistine casts upon the living God. With no boasting
words, but with steadfast reliance upon an Almighty arm,
he goes forth into the valley to meet the giant. He is girt
with no sword, he carries no spear or shield, he wears no
coat of armor — but he goes forth clad in the whole armor
of God, and has for his defense the shield of faith.

Was ever nobler word uttered by man than that which
David addressed to his adversary? What immovable
confidence has he in the name of the Lord! He says to the
Philistine, "You come to me with a sword and with a spear,
and with a shield — but I come to you in the name of the
Lord Almighty, the God of the armies of Israel, whom you
have defied. This day will the Lord deliver you into my
hand — and all this assembly shall know that the Lord

saves not with sword and spear; for the battle is the Lord's, and He will give you into our hands!"

We wait for the outcome. Not long need we delay. Goliath thinks to crush his youthful foe in a moment, as a man treads a worm beneath his feet — but never was he more deceived. The worm becomes the giant! David was weak — yet was he strong. His own arm was feeble, but he was strengthened by the arm of Omnipotence. So he slays the Gittite with the sling and the stone which he had despised, and cuts off the giant's head with the very sword in which he had trusted. So Israel triumphs, and Philistia is discomfited; and women come out of all the cities of Israel, singing the praises of the one who had thus saved their country from the enemy they feared. (1 Samuel 17.)

The narrative shows the strength which the Christian may look for in the conflict which he has to maintain. The servant of the Lord has ever a battle to fight. To no life of quiet ease, to no course of self-indulgent rest — is the Christian called. David warring with the giant is a true picture of the struggle for which each Christian must prepare. When a man is awakened by the Spirit to feel his exceeding sinfulness, he is invited at once to draw near to Christ. He is freely received, welcomed, loved, forgiven, the very moment that he thus in faith commits himself to the grace and mercy of the Savior. But as Christ sprinkles upon him His blood, He gives to him a uniform, and says to him: "Henceforth you are Mine! You are to serve Me, and fight my battles. Until death shall make your victory complete, you are to stand on my side, to witness for Me; and whatever opposes, to hold fast the banner of my cross in the midst of a hostile world!"

Then, like David, the Christian throws down the gauntlet. He withstands manfully the foes of Christ — the world, the flesh, and the devil. He finds the battlefield everywhere.

In his own heart and life has he to resist sins, evil passions, a rebellious will, pride, temper, sloth, selfishness, and all that is born of his own corrupt nature.

In the Church and in the world has he to stand firm in resisting error, in confessing his Master, and in endeavoring to bring over into the Lord's camp captives made willing in the day of His power.

But the story of David's conquest with Goliath, may also remind us of the utter disproportion between the strength of the Christian and that of his adversaries. What could be more striking than the contrast between the two combatants in the valley of Elah? The one was but a youth, and ruddy — the other in the full strength of mature manhood. The one was but a shepherd lad — the other a man of war. The one was but of small stature — the other a giant whose height was six cubits and a span. The one had no experience of the arts of warfare — the other had been accustomed to the battlefield for years. The one carried but a sling and a stone — the other was armed with a coat of armor. To have judged according to appearances, it must have seemed certain that the outcome of the conflict must have been disastrous to Israel. We would have said that but one result was possible — that the champion of Philistia must have gained the day, and that David must have been defeated and slain.

So great is the contrast also between the soldier of the Cross and the foes with whom he has to contend. On the one side is our adversary, the Devil, strong in his invisibility, striking a blow in the dark, when we look not for his approach — strong in the experience of past ages — strong in the legion of evil spirits who do his bidding — strong in the aid which is rendered by wicked men — strong in the power which the world exercises over us in its snares, in its example, in its reproach and persecutions — strong through the giant sins and passions of the flesh. And on the other side, how strengthless is the Christian in himself to overcome. How weak is the heart, how weak in purposing or in performing. Nor only is the Christian weak in other respects, but especially in this, that there is a warring party within the very citadel of his being. If by grace there is a better self that hates the evil and choose the good, that hungers after righteousness and longs to draw nearer to God, there is also another self — the old man that loves sin, cleaves to it, and holds out even to the end.

Let us endeavor to realize all this. It may teach us humility. It may teach us that we need moment by moment to look out of ourselves. It may teach us to be thoroughly in earnest, to watch always, and to be strong in the Lord, and in the power of His might; for it is thus that in spite of all we may defeat our foes, and be faithful unto death.

Once more look at David, and consider the secret of his confidence and strength. Look at the weapon he employed, and the spirit in which he used it. The sling and the stone seemed but a feeble means of resistance, yet was it mightier than the spear, the helmet, the shield, and the sword of Goliath; for David looked away from self, to the mighty power of God. He employed means, but he trusted not in them, but in the Rock of Israel. His eye was fixed on this one thing: "There is help in God, and there is help for me!" Thus he went forth to meet the foe, and thus he trampled him beneath his feet.

Our weapons are simple as David's, yet are they sufficient when we handle them in the name of the Lord. "The weapons of our warfare are not carnal, but mighty through God to the pulling down of strong-holds." Prayer and the Word are two of the chief weapons with which the Christian fights. They are as the sling and stone — but feeble to the eye of sense, yet through God their power is invincible. They were the secret spring of that noble valor which David displayed before the eyes of all Israel. Only read the utterances of his heart in the Psalms; see how perpetually he sought help from above; how he cried unto the Lord with his whole heart. See how in God's Word he comforted himself, and made His testimonies his meditation day and night, and then without wavering trusted only in the Lord — and we are at no loss to understand why he was fearless — when all beside were in terror, and why he conquered — when not an Israelite in all the army dare accept the challenge of Goliath.

In this confidence likewise may the Christian prove more than a match for all that opposes.

True, the adversary is strong;
true, the temptations of the world are strong;
true, there are giant sins, lusts, passions to be overcome;
true, your own strength is nothing.

But hide God's Word in your heart, rejoice in its promises, and cheerfully follow the leading of its precepts — and inner strength will thus be imparted.

Moreover, keep near the throne of grace; let your feet often tread the slopes of Olivet; pray in the morning, and pray in the evening; pray in your own secret chamber, and pray in spirit even when in the throng of business or society. Pray without ceasing, ever looking unto Jesus as your Righteousness, your Mediator, and your faithful High Priest — and then you will be secure. No weapon that is formed against you shall prosper, but you shall abide in safe-guard with your King. "Trust in the Lord forever, for in the Lord Jehovah is everlasting strength!"

There is another narrative of Holy Scripture that illustrates in another direction, the subject which engages our attention. We find it given in 2 Corinthians 12. The Apostle of the Gentiles had been permitted to behold such a glory, and to hear such unspeakable words, that he might have been exalted above measure through the abundance of the revelations which he had received. So a thorn in the flesh, the messenger of Satan, comes to buffet him, to try him, to keep him low in self-abasement before God. Whatever it may have been, whether weakness of sight, feebleness of utterance, or some other distressing infirmity — it was a sore trial, and most earnestly does he entreat God that it may be removed.

Perhaps in remembrance of the thrice offered petition in Gethsemane, three times does he beseech the Lord that it may depart from him. But as the bitter cup of death was not taken away from the Savior, but fresh grace and strength were bestowed — so was it also with Paul. The affliction, remained, but a most gracious promise was given: "My grace is sufficient for you, for my strength is made perfect in weakness."

Then the Apostle no more prays for the removal of the trial, but joyfully, gladly bears the cross laid upon him. "Most gladly," he declares, "will I rather glory in my infirmities, that the power of Christ may rest upon me. Therefore I take pleasure in infirmities, in reproaches, in necessities, in persecutions, in distresses, for Christ's sake — for when I am weak, then am I strong."

We see here the strength promised and given for the endurance of trial and affliction. It is lawful and right, yes, it is commanded, that in the day of trouble we should call upon the Lord, and seek the lightening or removal of our grief of Him. But we must leave it to His infinite wisdom to answer the petition in the best way. He may give us, and give us speedily, exactly what we seek; if not, the prayer shall be no less answered; for if He takes not the burden away — He will impart of His own strength, that we may be able to bear it.

Very rich and full is the promise, "My grace is sufficient for you, for My strength is made perfect in weakness." It has been spoken of as an elastic promise. The word "sufficient" may not sound very great, but it stretches according to a man's necessity. A man's need may be great today — and the Word reaches it. It may be ten times as great tomorrow — but the Word reaches it still. The grace is still sufficient for the greater need — as for the lesser.

The promise shows also that not until we are weak, does the Lord bestow His strength. We may be too strong for the Lord to help us. Gideon's army must be brought almost to nothing before the Lord will use it to overthrow the Midianites. And until we are brought low in our own thoughts, until the discipline employed has thoroughly emptied us of all high imaginings as to what we can do, or we can effect, or we can bear — we cannot be strong in the Lord.

"Though I am nothing." 2 Corinthians 12:11

Wonderful was the grace that taught the once proud Pharisee thus to speak!

To be "the least of the apostles," was much to say. (1 Corinthians 15:9)

To be "less than the least of all all God's people," was still more. (Ephesians 3:8)

To be "chief of sinners," was yet more. (1 Timothy 1:15)

But "to be nothing," this is the very acme of humility!

"God opposes the proud, but gives grace to the humble." James 4:6"When I am weak," and not before, "then am I strong." (2 Corinthians 12:10.) When I have learned experimentally that I am a bruised reed, that I have in myself no power to endure affliction, that left to myself I shall assuredly rebel against the rod and murmur against the gracious Hand that holds it — then the Lord draws near by the Spirit, and gives a joy, a peace that nothing can destroy.

Perhaps nowhere do we see more the strength of Jesus manifested in weakness, than in the steadfastness of our Protestant martyrs, when called on to suffer for the truth's sake.

We have a touching account of the last days of Anne Askew, a lady of high position, who endured the flames of martyrdom in the year 1546. She wrote before her death: "Written by me, Anne Askew, who neither desires death, nor fears its might, and am as merry as one bound to Heaven. She was placed on the rack for two long hours, while the Lord Chancellor persuaded her in vain to renounce the truth.

Unable to walk or stand from the tortures she had suffered, she was carried in a chair to Smithfield and fastened to the stake. One who saw her there declared that she had "an angel's countenance and a smiling face." At the very last, a written pardon was offered to her if she would recant, but she turned away her eyes and would not look at it. "She did not come there," she said, "to deny her Lord and Master." Thus compassed in the flames, as a blessed sacrifice to God, she slept in the Lord, leaving behind her a singular example of Christian steadfastness for all men to follow.

The following beautiful prayer she has left behind: "O Lord, I have more enemies now than there be hairs on my head! Yet Lord, let them never overcome me with vain words — for on You I cast my care! With all the spite they can imagine, they fall upon me, who am Your poor creature. Yet, sweet Lord, let me not regard those who are against me — for in You is my whole delight. And, Lord, I heartily desire of You that in Your most merciful goodness, will forgive them that violence which they do and have done unto me. Open their blind hearts, that they may hereafter do that thing in Your sight which is only acceptable before You, and to set forth Your verity aright without all vain fantasies of sinful men. So be it, O Lord, so be it."

"She kept her faith in God, enduring shame and agony with meek, unshaken constancy. None but Christ, none but Christ could have made the weakness of a delicate woman so strong — the feebleness of a mortal creature so triumphant!"

Let the Christian take hold of the strength promised, let him lean only upon it without faltering, remembering that otherwise he is unable so much as to purpose or perform one single action, or to cherish one single thought that is pleasing to God. And then let him strive to the very uttermost to glorify God both in body and spirit, let him go forth into the world's highway as the servant of Christ to win souls, to maintain the truth, to bear witness for His Master.

Shall we not in this crisis of our Church's history, arise to take a higher view of our duties and responsibilities? Shall we not cast aside . . .
   our self-pleasing,
   our love of ease,
   our resting in home comforts,
   our expensive tastes and habits,
   our conformity to the standard of the world
   — and go forth with self-denying effort,
   praying more frequently,
   working even to weariness,
   giving that which costs us something,
   enduring hardness as good soldiers of Jesus Christ?

Until there is more of this among us, there is little hope of making an effectual stand on behalf of Christ's truth. Were Christian people to do it, assuredly God would put forth His power, and the Gospel would again triumph as in days of old.

Not long ago I asked a missionary lately returned from Africa, what means they had found most effectual to win over the heathen to the cause of Christ. He answered that the greatest success was obtained when the heathen saw our missionaries working miracles — that is, as he explained, performing acts of kindness and love altogether unlike anything to which they have been accustomed, and which their own principles could never enable them to do. Would that we had more such miracle-workers among ourselves! Such self-denying kindness, such sincere charity must tell powerfully wherever it is found.

But I would speak to those who have not as yet peace with God. Be sure there can be no strength in God, unless first you have peace with God. While sin lies heavy on the spirit, while there is a conscience ill at ease, while an alienated heart remains, and the thought of meeting God in judgment is terrible — how can you possibly be strong to overcome temptation or to meet the sorrows that may befall you? The thought of God's presence in this case must be a source of fear and disquietude rather than of strength and consolation.

Reader, seek above all things, as you go forth to meet the unknown future, to know assuredly that the great account is settled, that sin is forgiven through the blood of the Cross, and that whatever happens, God is on your side.

Only hearken to the message of the PAST. Is there not many a blank in your parish, in your neighborhood, and perhaps a vacant place at your own fireside? Have you not lost someone whom you knew, perhaps one very dear to you — a parent, a child, a brother, a sister, a friend? And if you have, does not a voice from their grave seem to chide you, and that in no uncertain tone, for your delay in seeking the Lord?

And can you not look back on a gracious Hand stretched out to preserve and deliver you? Many others have died — and why not you? Fatal accidents have come — but you have escaped. Dangerous diseases have spread their snares around — but you have escaped. Must you not say, "It is of the Lord's mercies we are not consumed, because His compassions fail not"? And what is the voice of each merciful deliverance — but a call to return back at once to God?

Then look forward to the FUTURE. Think of its probabilities. If you are at all in the habit of looking at things as they really are, and not as your own fancies or wishes would paint them — there are few readers but must see many things highly probable which would yet be very hard to meet if they really happened. There may be a dark and gloomy cloud hanging over your own immediate circle of interest — and you cannot possibly tell how it may break. It may be with respect to your own health, symptoms may appear which tell you plainly that it is declining. Or it may be the health of another which causes you much anxiety. Or it may be difficulties in your calling, or circumstances connected with your business or your little store of capital, that look threatening. Something of this, you may be obliged to confess: something you fear very probably, or at least very possibly, may occur within a short period. And if it should be so, how can you meet it unless you are resting on the Rock, so that the waves and storms of affliction and trial shall beat against you in vain?

Reader, why will you not now, even now, return home to your Father's house? Why not now accept the free salvation which is so graciously offered to you in Christ?

Is not the time past long enough to have lived in the far country?

Have you not trespassed long enough on the patience and forbearance of the Most High God?

Have you not long enough rejected the Savior and grieved the Spirit?

Have you not long enough been treading the road that leads to destruction?

Think of all the evil that has stained the years that are passed, and let the sight of it impel you to go at once to the only Fountain opened for sin! Think of the present blessedness of those that are in Christ, and make it all your own by earnest and believing supplication to Him. Think of the glories of the future kingdom, and the everlasting security of His people! You shall partake of it all — if only you now come back as a wandering sheep to His fold, and henceforth follow in the footsteps of the good Shepherd.

Oh, hear the solemn voice of the Son of Man now calling to you as if by name: "Child of this world, who lingers so near the brink of everlasting woe, awake! awake, before the shadows of night fall upon you. The night is hastening on apace when no man can work, when your feet will stumble on the dark mountains. The past cannot be undone — but its guilt may now be forgiven you. The future lies before you — use it for God, employ well the talents that He has given you. Make haste to live — before it is the time to die. Whatever your hand finds to do, do it with all your might. Let the goodness of the Lord lead you to repentance. Let your soul rest on Christ for righteousness and strength. Evermore abide in the love and fear of God."

O God, the strength of all those who put their trust in You, mercifully accept our prayers; and because through the weakness of our mortal nature we can do no good thing without You — grant us the help of Your grace, that in keeping of Your commandments we may please You both in will and deed; through Jesus Christ our Lord. Amen.

Deepen the Well!

By all means deepen the well! The water is earthy and brackish — the supply is scanty — therefore, go deeper! Take spade and pick-axe — remove the soil — and by and by the water will spring up more fresh, more pure, more abundant.

But what is this well? There is a deep, unfathomable Well-spring of grace and mercy in Christ. He is the Well of Life — He is the very Fountain of Living Waters. This Well needs no deepening. Yesterday, today, and forever, it is full to overflowing, for all who resort to it.

But there is another well. Those who receive of Christ this living water become themselves little wells, little fountains, having in their hearts this grace, and thence becoming sources of blessing to others; by their words and prayers and Christian example, passing on to those around them the good they themselves have received.

We have the promise of the Old Testament, (Isaiah 58:11): "You shall be like a spring of water, whose waters fail not." And this promise is confirmed and explained by Christ Himself (John 4:14): "Whoever drinks of the water that I shall give him shall never thirst, but the water that I shall give him shall be in him a well of water springing up into everlasting life." So again in John 7:37, 38: "If anyone is thirsty, let him come to me and drink. Whoever believes in me, as the Scripture has said, streams of living water will flow from within him."

Here is true spiritual life. The living water, the grace of the blessed Spirit of God, the indwelling of the Holy Spirit revealing . . .

sin in all its terrible deformity;

God in His holiness, justice, mercy, and truth;

Christ as all-sufficient to meet every need of the soul — the only Savior, able to save to the uttermost them that come to God by Him — by means of the truth permeating the whole spiritual man — the mind, the memory, the will, the affections, the imagination; and thus quickening, sanctifying, elevating man, and making him meet for the inheritance of the saints in light.

It is well to distinguish true spiritual life from its COUNTERFEITS.

There may be the gift of utterance — and no spiritual life. Balaam, and Judas, and multitudes beside have had this — and yet have been dead in trespasses and sins. "Though I speak with the tongue of men and angels, and have not love" (one of the blessed graces of the Spirit), "I am only a resounding gong or a clanging cymbal." Men may offer fine prayers before others, men may preach eloquent sermons — and yet be far from God.

The most wicked man, the most consummate hypocrite I ever knew — was one of the most gifted preachers, and could electrify an audience by his persuasive oratory.

There may be participation in outward ordinances — and yet no spiritual life. The principle of Romans 2:28, 29, applies to all ages of the Church's history: "A man is not a Jew if he is only one outwardly, nor is circumcision merely outward and physical. No, a man is a Jew if he is one inwardly; and circumcision is circumcision of the heart, by the Spirit, not by the written code. Such a man's praise is not from men, but from God."

Ever remember that it is only when sacraments are rightly received, that they bring a blessing from God. Who can tell the numbers who frequent the table of the Lord — and yet never feed on Him in their hearts by faith?

There may be emotion, the manifestation of deep feeling — and yet no spiritual life. There is often . . .
    a devout frame of mind under a fervent sermon,
    or the stirring of the heart under the sound of sweet music,
    or convictions of danger at some solemn season.

And yet this may prove a temporary breath of religiousness, which has no root, and no lasting effect.

There may be outward separation from the world — and yet no spiritual life. There may be an ascetic life — years passed in a nunnery or monastery — and this may be the working of a self-righteous spirit, striving to obtain by mortification of the flesh, the pardon which God loves to bestow as the free gift of His unspeakable love.

Or there may be in Evangelical circles, an abstinence from all that the world calls pleasure — and yet the love of the Father perchance is not reigning supreme within the heart.

There may be great activity in the Lord's vineyard — and yet no spiritual life. It is much easier to be active workers — than to be constant in prayer, and living a life of faith before God. The Church of Sardis by her labors had a name to live, but she was dead.

And may there not sometimes be a forced activity to silence conscience, and this just because there is no life — a cloak to cover your dead soul festering in its corruption?

It seems to me that the one chief feature of the spiritual life is this — Christ is a great reality to the living soul. Once He was but a name — but One at a very far distance — One perhaps feared as a Judge, or regarded as One we might fall back upon by-and-by, when the world had lost its attraction. But now how changed is all this!

Perhaps, dear reader, this was your view a short time ago; but God has been of late teaching you precious lessons, and now old things have passed away — and all things have become new.

Christ is now to you a Friend dearer than those you love best on earth.

His friends are your friends.

His name fills your heart with unspeakable joy.

You look to Him for all grace and help and strength.

You love to think of His promises.

His presence is your resource in solitude or in trial.

You love to work for Him, and to lay at His feet all you possess, to be employed in His happy service.

His Word has become to you a new book. It speaks to your very heart, and reminds you continually of His love.

You can say in a measure with Paul, "Christ lives in me: and the life I now live in the flesh I live by the faith in the Son of God, who loved me and gave Himself for me! To me to live is Christ — to die is gain."

A dying Christian in India was telling of her hope.
She put her hand on her Bible, and she said, "I have Christ here!"
And then she put her hand near her heart, and she said, "I have Christ here!"
And then she pointed up to Heaven, and said, "I have Christ there!"

Such is the spiritual life of which I speak. "This is life eternal, to know You the only true God, and Jesus Christ whom You have sent."

Reader, is this life yours? Dead men cannot abide long in the house of the living. "Give me a burying-place," said Abraham, "that I may bury my dead out of my sight." Thus dead souls cannot dwell in glory with living saints. There must be a separation.

Are you dead in sins? Christ's voice calls you: Awake and live! Come forth from the grave of your sins this very hour, and Christ is near to give you light and life!

Perhaps in the heart of some reader of this little book there may of late have been awakened a desire for this spiritual life — and yet you feel uncertain how to obtain it. Take it as a certain truth, that the way is very simple, and the blessing very near. Look at it in this light: Christ stands at your door; His heart full of love and compassion, His hands are full of gifts, having for you the gift of repentance, pardon, and the grace of His Spirit, and longing to bestow them upon you. Some go on for years, asking and praying in an unbelieving sort of spirit — and then wonder that they do not find comfort. Why, friend, it is not so much your prayer to Christ, as for you to see that Jesus is entreating you to accept His love and mercy and salvation, entreating you to let Him enter the sanctuary of your heart, and there to dwell; bestowing on you all the blessings of His friendship, of reconciliation with God, and of the new life of holiness and love.

Hearken to those words of the Apostle, "Now then we are ambassadors for Christ, as though God did beseech you by us: we beg you in Christ's stead, be reconciled to God."

You must take His outstretched hand; you must, in a believing spirit, look to Him for that which He delights to bestow. Your prayer is not to be the difficult task of obtaining from One unwilling to give — but the blessed, happy, joyful one, of heartily receiving the unspeakable benefit which your best Friend loves to grant to you.

If you want this spiritual life, don't fix your eye on Self in any shape — neither your prayer, nor your sense of need, nor your repentance, nor your faith; all this is utterly deficient, and will make you ready to despair. But look up to Him who delights to give all — grace to pray, grace to repent, grace to trust; and He will honor your confidence, and exceed all your thoughts in the richness and abundance of His bounty.

But if you are already in possession of true spiritual life in Christ, there is need of its evermore being deepened. There needs a greater realization of divine things, a fuller life, a more abundant influx of grace from the Fountainhead. You may be sure that the deeper the life . . .
the more full will be the joy,
the more will you be able to glorify God, and
the greater your usefulness in His service.

It is not so much increase of gifts that we need, as increase of grace to make us vessels fit for the Master's use and prepared for every good work.

Very certain it is likewise, that the best way to prevent a relapse into worldly habits, and a return to a cold and lukewarm spirit — is to make continual progress in the Divine life, to strive after higher attainments, and to drink deeper into the ocean of Divine love.

Very strongly would I urge upon any who have lately set out in the Christian life, never to relax their efforts to obtain more and more grace and life in Christ. I know of nothing more sorrowful than to see a young Christian, at first very zealous and prayerful, slipping back little by little into habits of worldliness or inconsistency — instead of going from strength to strength, and each year and each month manifesting more evidently the blessed fruits of the indwelling Spirit.

But how may you deepen your Christian life?

(1) Keep clear and distinct the blessed truth that your acceptance and justification before God, are not dependent upon the measure of spiritual life which you possess.

If you wish to have a deepening spiritual life, take care not to confound your justification with the sanctifying grace which dwells in you. For the growth of the inner life as well as for our peace, the eye must rest on Christ alone. He alone is your Ransom, your Substitute, your Righteousness before the throne of God. You never can enjoy the least assurance of pardon, or sense of fellowship with God — unless the ground of it is altogether independent of yourself.

Only consider how great is your guiltiness; what utter unworthiness, what sins, deficiencies, failings in everything, would bar all approach to a just and holy God, were it not that you have a plea which cannot be gainsaid.

A bride was passing out of the Church where she had just been married, and a friend threw down a few flowers at the feet of the newly married couple. A few drops of the water in which the flowers had been kept, touched the bride's dress, and shortly after a tiny speck was noticed upon it. "A spot of sin as small as this, would shut either of us out of Heaven," was the remark made.

But as seen by the eye of a heart-searching God, what numberless foul blots and stains defile the robe of each of us! and how could we then appear before Him unless clothed in the immaculate Righteousness which He has provided through the merits and death of His well-beloved Son?

But when casting off all trust in self — in converted self as well as unconverted self — we repose all our confidence in Christ our Righteousness, we can then enjoy peace with God, and seek at His footstool increase of all spiritual blessings.

In St. Stephen's Church, Carlisle, I noticed a memorial erected to the late Rev. Waldegrave, having engraved upon it an extract from his will, executed shortly before his death, and which testifies the blessed consolation this hope affords. "I desire in the first place to testify that I die in the faith of Christ crucified, and as a sinner saved by grace alone, humbly trusting in the alone blood and righteousness of my Lord and Savior Jesus Christ, and in the full assurance of that eternal and unchangeable love of the Father, Son, and Holy Spirit, one Triune God, which it has been my joy and delight to have been permitted to proclaim throughout my beloved diocese, and which doctrines, as they have been my comfort in life are now my stay and support in the prospect of death and eternity; and I commend all those over whom I have had the oversight, both pastors and flocks, to God and to the Word of His grace."

(2) We may deepen spiritual life by gaining clearer views of our own depravity in the light of God's holiness and majesty.

JOB was a true man. He was accepted by God. He walked before Him in sincerity and uprightness. But in his earlier life there was but a partial knowledge of himself and his sin. But the well was deepened. His sore afflictions brought him much nearer to God. He learned to regard sin in a far different light. He learned to see his own life under the piercing ray of the Divine glory. Then he was humbled

in the dust. "I have heard of You by the hearing of the ear
— but now my eye sees You. Therefore I abhor myself, and
repent in dust and ashes!"

It was thus with the Prophet ISAIAH. He had a vision
of Jehovah sitting on His throne. He heard the seraphim
cry, "Holy, holy, holy, Lord God of hosts." Then came the
overwhelming conviction of His own defilement: "Woe is
me, for I am undone; because I am a man of unclean lips,
and I dwell in the midst of a people of unclean lips; for my
eyes have seen the King, the Lord Almighty!" There was a
deepening of the well, more experience of the reality and
evil of sin, and afterward a fuller joy in the sense of its
forgiveness.

Oh, Christians, let us strive to get into God's light! Let
us more realize His solemn Presence, His Holiness, His
Majesty. Let us enter into the experience of Psalm 139. In
God's presence let us seek to lay bare our inmost thoughts
and ways. Let us cast away all covering and excuse, and
desire above everything to know ourselves as He sees us to
be: "Search me, O God, and know my heart; try me, and
know my thoughts, and see if there is any way of
wickedness in me, and lead me in the way everlasting."

(3) Deepen the spiritual life by avoiding all that
checks and impedes its flow, and by diligent use of all the
means of grace which God has appointed for its increase. A
recent historian has described the course of the two great
rivers, the Tigris and the Euphrates. He tells how the one
loses much of its waters in the marshy lands through which
it flows, and reaches the mouth with far less body and
depth of water than it possessed in an earlier part of its
course. But the Tigris presents a great contrast to this. It
retains the water it possessed in its earlier course; while

receiving tributaries on both sides, it grows deeper and
fuller as it empties its waters into the sea.

Thus it is with two Christians. The one loses much life
and comfort and grace in the marshy lands of uncertain
doctrine, of unscriptural views, of worldly conformity. Ah,
the river grows very shallow . . .

when luxury and ease and self-pleasing bear sway;

when the tongue is full of every name but the One
Name;

when the claims of business supersede the claims of
God's kingdom;

when doubtful maxims are followed instead of the
plain precepts of the Word;

when eagerness to obtain more wealth shuts up the
hand that once was liberal;

when the safe rule of avoiding scenes of temptation
relaxes little by little.

Nor less is the danger to the spiritual life when
unscriptural expedients are made use of to promote it. The
Holy Spirit is the bestower of all real spiritual life. He also
is the Author of the Holy Scriptures, which He has given
that the man of God may be perfect, thoroughly furnished
unto all good works. And we may be sure that He will
never work by means opposed to the spirit of that Word.
When men resort to habitual confession to a priest, instead
of laying bare the heart to Him who searches the thoughts;
or when men go out of the world and take monastic vows;
or when a multitude of ceremonies and self-imposed
ordinances distract the thoughts and burden the conscience
— these things in the end will rather hinder than forward
the life of the soul, because they lead away from the close
spiritual fellowship with the Father and the Son, which
above all things is essential.

With another Christian it is very different. The stream of spiritual life deepens day by day, and week by week. Like the river Tigris, he gets help from tributary streams. He gains assistance from all those precious means of grace which Christ has appointed to refresh us in our pilgrimage.

Oh, Christian, be zealous to improve these merciful provisions of our gracious Father!

Take deeper draughts of the river of Divine truth. Go to Holy Scripture with a prayer and determination to understand more of its revelations of Christ, of your eternal inheritance, of your own position of privilege and responsibility. Let the word of Christ dwell in you richly in all wisdom.

Take the old promises and encouragements with which you have been familiar for years, and by devout meditation upon them, by placing them close beside your own sins, and fears, and necessities — see if they do not stand out in fresh life and power.

Take, again, other portions, such as the Book of the Chronicles, or the minor Prophets, with which perhaps you have been less familiar, and carefully examine them until you find food for thought which perhaps you little expected.

Let there be more of the spirit of prayer. Let there be more reality in the assurance that God is very near at hand, that each prayer-word in Jesus' name is a power-word, that sooner shall the throne of God be shaken than that a single believing petition offered by the weakest or most unworthy suppliant miss the mark, or fail of securing the best answer.

Let there be more fellowship and communion with God's people. Greatly do most Christians lose the profit they might gain from this. Oh, that we could get rid of the stiffness and formality and cold civilities that too often take the place of the hearty, loving fellowship on the things of God, that ought to exist. Dear reader, try to break down this stone wall that separates one Christian heart from another, and hinders many a word of help, many a prayer, many a suggestion for some new labor of love in the Lord's Vineyard.

Let there be a frequent drawing near to the holy table. There renew your covenant with God; there gain fresh views of Christ's dying love; there feed in faith on that body broken, and that blood shed on the cross for you.

Let there be a constant effort to give back in blessing to others the grace and consolation which God has given you. In giving to others — we receive more from God. "He who waters — shall be watered." We ought not to be like the Dead Sea, which receives unto itself the flow of the Jordan, but gives nothing in return. Rather should we be like the Sea of Galilee, which receives at its northern extremity, and then gives forth at its southern. I am sure there is a blessing in striving to impart to others the knowledge of salvation.

A few years ago, a young man went out to India in the civil service, because he felt scarcely prepared for the solemn responsibility of entering the ministry of the Church. At an outstation in India where he was stationed, a dying soldier spent a few weeks before his course was run. The young man felt it his duty to go and read to him, and teach him as far as he knew of the Word of God. His hours spent by that sick bed were the happiest of his life. He learned to see the love of Christ as he had never seen it before. To use his own language — in trying to convert the soldier, God converted him, as well as fulfilled his desire to be useful to the dying man.

Let Christians remember, too, how guilty will they be in holding back the knowledge from others by which alone they can be saved. I have heard that a member of the medical profession, in commencing practice, has to take a solemn oath that if ever he should discover any medicine likely to be largely beneficial to mankind — he will not withhold the discovery, but declare it openly for the general benefit. And if we have been taught the value of that blessed remedy for human guilt, the precious blood of the cross — shall we hesitate to do our best everywhere to make it known among others?

DEEPEN THE WELL! Yes — why should we not? Why be content with a scanty measure of blessing — when the fountain is so full? "I am come that they might have life, and that they might have it more abundantly." And if the purpose of Christ's coming is thus to give more abundantly — will He refuse a large supply of Divine grace to a soul that thirsts after it?

We have an example of such longings in the Book of Psalms. "As the deer pants after the water-brooks — so pants my soul after You, O God." "My soul thirsts for God, for the living God — when shall I come and appear before God?" "O God, You are my God — early will I seek You. My soul thirsts for You, my flesh longs for You in a dry and thirsty land, where there is no water." "Whom have I in Heaven but You? And there is none upon earth that I desire beside You!"

It would prove of great help to Christians if they would endeavor often, amidst the busy duties of life, to stir up their hearts in such desires and meditations as these. They bring a rich reward. God satisfies the longing soul, and fills the hungry soul with goodness. "Blessed are those who hunger and thirst after righteousness, for they shall be filled."

But very especially would I ask the attention of the reader to the prayers of the Apostle Paul as presenting to us, in a most instructive form, the longing of Christian hearts for more of this spiritual life. Look at Paul's prayer for the Roman Christians: "Now may the God of hope fill you with all joy and peace in believing, that you may abound in hope through the power of the Holy Spirit."

We look up to God Himself. He, the God of hope, the God of peace, the God of all grace — delights to send the power of His Spirit to fill the souls of His poor needy children with a heavenly joy, an abiding peace, an aspiring hope. And it is in the way of believing that we can enjoy this. Trusting in Him who is the Root and Offspring of David, as in the previous verse, the Holy Spirit bestows a joy which is unspeakable.

But look also at the prayer of the Apostle for the Ephesians. (Ephesians 3:14-21.) I know no description like it of a deep spiritual life within the soul. And now just glance at this exquisite prayer, one we should do well often to use on our knees before God when asking for more depth in our religion: "I bow my knees unto the Father of our Lord Jesus Christ" (what sweet confidence is here — the Father of Christ — hence my Father in Him).

"That He would grant you according to the riches of His glory." Here is the treasury from which comes our supply. His own glorious riches — His all-sufficient grace. His own hand full of all goodness and bounty.

"To be strengthened with might by His Spirit in the inner man." Or, as in Colossians 1:10, "Strengthened with all might, according to His glorious power." The Holy Spirit raising the soul above its own native feebleness, conferring an energy, a secret force enabling it to resist temptation, to bear sorrow, to toil and labor in the vineyard.

"That Christ may dwell in your hearts by faith." The shrine, the sanctuary filled with a vivid realization of the Lord's presence with His child, and this in the exercise of continual reliance upon Him.

"That you, being rooted and grounded in love, may be able to comprehend with all saints what is the breadth, and length, and depth, and height; and to know the love of Christ, which passes knowledge." Here the idea is the tree with the roots going deep into the ground of God's love, or the building resting on the immovable basis of that love — and then the soul learning out little by little that which will ever surpass all possibility of comprehension. High is the Heaven, deep is Hell, broad is the sea, long is eternity — but higher, and deeper, and broader, and longer, is Christ's love — and blessed is it to reach after the knowledge of it, though we must ever fall short.

"That you might be filled with all the fullness of God." Ah, what an abounding fullness here! Compare Colossians 1:19: "It pleased the Father that in Him should all fullness dwell;" and Colossians 2:9, 10: "For in Christ all the fullness of the Deity lives in bodily form, and you have been given fullness in Christ, who is the head over every power and authority!" which seems the right rendering of the passage.

Here is a supply out of which to draw. Deepen the well! Yes, you may indeed. You are not straitened in the Lord, but in yourself — in your low desires, in your unbelief, in your lack of prayer. For it is prayer which gains all — the prayer which springs from faith. Unspeakably great as is the measure of blessing referred to in this passage — yet mark how the Apostle closes it. "Now unto Him that is able to do exceeding abundantly above all that we ask or think, according to the power that works in us, unto Him be glory in the Church by Christ Jesus, throughout all ages world without end. Amen."

Nearer to Thee

Communion with God is the greatest reality of the
Christian life. It is the soul of all true religion. "That which
we have heard and seen, we declare unto you — and truly
our fellowship is with the Father and with His Son Jesus
Christ." Such words as these are not the words of an
enthusiast — they are the calm and sober statement of a
great and blessed fact. They tell of the abiding peace and
consolation of the aged Apostle who penned them. He had
known much of persecution. He had tasted the weariness
and solitude of exile in Patmos. He had experienced
sorrowful partings from friends beloved.

But in the midst of all he had peace. He had the joy of
close, intimate, felt fellowship and fellowship with Him
who is the fountain of all true blessedness. It is as if he
would say, "I have friends of which none can rob me; I
have society from which no exile can debar me; I have
companionship which fills my soul with truest gladness.
Would that all you to whom I write might share with me
the sweetness of this heavenly fellowship!"

The echo of these words of John is heard in many a
heart. There are multitudes of men and women engaged in
lowly toil and the commonest avocations, who yet know
what is meant by fellowship with God. They see One whom
others see not. They hear One whom others hear not. They
walk along earth's highway, delighting in God, calling upon
His name, and strengthened by the joy of His covenant
presence in Christ.

And when we begin to look onwards into the future,
what is the desire that should be awakened, and the wish
that we most should cherish? There is much we might

desire as to the work we have to do, or as to the evils that we deplore. There is much ploughing, and sowing, and weeding, and reaping, to be carried on in the Lord's vineyard, and all this we would gladly do better than we have before. But the Christian desires more than this. He would reach after greater nearness to the Source of all holiness and peace. The language of the inner spirit is this: "It is good for me to draw near to God; yes, I would draw nearer and nearer, until I see Your unveiled glory, and be forever with You where You are!"

> Nearer, my God, to Thee — nearer to Thee,
> E'en though it be a cross that raises me!
> Yet all my song shall be,
> Nearer, my God, to Thee — nearer to Thee.

There are two special reasons from the character of the times in which our lot is cast, why each Christian should more than ever cultivate communion with God.

The intense activity of the day is a reason for it. Many run to and fro. The world is all alive. There is little time for quietness and thought. There is a constant rushing hither and thither. Men crowd double the amount of work into the same time of labor. Men's brains are on the rack to discover new inventions or new ways of making gain, to keep pace with the times in which they live. But is there no danger here? Is there no reason for special watchfulness? You may be too busy. You may have too many engagements. You may be keeping the vineyard of others — when you ought to be tending your own. Oh, take heed not to push piety into a corner! At all hazards make time for meditation, for Bible reading, and for prayer!

There can be no true communion with God, without setting carefully apart a definite time for it. Needs there not be a calmness and stillness of soul — the closing of the door, the retirement into self, the half-hour alone? And is not this too often forgotten? Do not the claims of work and business and outdoor duties infringe too much upon the quiet retreat of the prayer closet? Reader, be sure that you give time to God. Deny yourself, if it be necessary, and rise an hour earlier in the morning. What, if perchance the nursling of Divine grace in your soul should fade and wither and die for lack of the still hour, when the dew of Heaven might revive and renew it?

The other reason for special watchfulness I would name, is the painful amount of error, division, and controversy in the Christian Church. This becomes a sad stumbling-block to those who are on the outside, and who make it an excuse for their neglect. But it is a great stumbling-block also to Christians. Instead of living upon the essential truths of the faith, men are compelled to spend their time in endeavoring to uphold and defend them. More than this — Christian men often mistake bitterness and wrath, for zeal. They forget that the wrath of man works not the righteousness of God. In this way, communion with God is hindered. Troubled waters cannot reflect the bright stars above — even so the mind full of controversy finds it very difficult to grow calm in the presence of its God, and thus gain something of His mind and Spirit.

The arena of disputation is not favorable for promoting spirituality of mind. It is easier to contend for a favorite opinion, yes, even for God's truth — than to bend the knee in fervent prayer. Many a zealous controversialist, on the right side and on the wrong, may be shut out from God's kingdom at last. God forbid that I should hinder one faithful witness for God's truth, or one clear denunciation of soul-destroying error. Yet watch over your own spirit. Be bold as the lion — as wise as the serpent — and withal, as gentle and harmless as the dove. Above all, keep close to God. Watch and pray, lest communion with God should grow cold and languid, while controversy waxes hotter and hotter.

He who lives in the atmosphere of continual prayer, like Stephen of old, will best know how to speak forth God's truth with a wisdom and power that the adversary cannot gainsay or resist.

In urging Christian people to a closer communion with God, it is needful to bear in mind several foundation principles.

1. Communion with God rests upon the affinity between the Divine and human natures. All possibility of this fellowship rests upon the fact that God created man in His own image. There is a power of going beyond that which is present and visible. There is a power of knowing and understanding something of the glory of the great Creator. There is a wonderful faculty of prayer, of holding converse with One unseen.

Strange theories are abroad with reference to man's origin, that would regard him as but little raised above the lower creation — but there is an infinite gulf of difference. The reproofs of conscience, the knowledge of good and evil, above all, man's religiousness, his need under all conditions of an object of worship, and when rightly directed, the power of rising in heart and mind to a true fellowship with Jehovah — all this testifies whence he comes.

Surely, then, if God has granted us this high prerogative, we ought diligently to use it. Let us not neglect our talent — let us not forget our noblest distinction. No plainer command has God given us, or one which it is a greater privilege to obey, than this: "You shall worship the Lord your God." The man who lives without prayer and buries his thoughts in present things, like Esau — sells his birthright for a mess of pottage. He voluntarily comes down from his high elevation, and reckons himself on a level with the beasts that perish.

2. There can be no communion except by means of a revelation given by God Himself. When man first was made, Jehovah condescended to hold communion with him. He delighted in the work of His own hands; and He drew near to those who were a reflection of His own spirituality, holiness, and love. But the breach came — the terrible catastrophe that snapped asunder this close tie of fellowship. Man shrinks now from the presence of his Maker; the attribute of an inflexible Justice frowns upon the rebel. Adam is immediately driven from Eden — a separation is made — the dark cloud of sin has raised a barrier between the frail child of dust and the great Creator.

What can be done? There, far away out of sight, is the great, glorious, all-holy Jehovah. Here is a sinner whose whole life is but a defiled garment, whose whole heart and nature are averse to His holiness, and fearful of His judgment.

How can they meet? All mere natural religion leaves an infinite chasm between the Creator and the creature, and leaves me but an atom in a vast universe — God far away — the great, the awful Judge, the Almighty.

All mere human theories, philosophies, wise teachings of learned men, can do nothing for me. They can speak of conforming to the law and order of the universe, but they cannot help me to get near to God. They can scarce tell me if there be a God; still less if He hears prayer; still less if He can forgive the sinner.

But Scripture revelation speaks with authority;
    it bridges over that vast chasm between me and my Creator;
    it brings near the promise of mercy and reconciliation;
    it bids me draw near to God, with the assurance that He will draw near to me;
    it tells me that a guilty monarch in his prison cell (King Manasseh) found the ear of Mercy open, and that an outcast woman was freely welcomed by a Redeemer's love.

Men speak of holding communion with God in nature. Go and behold the snow-capped mountains, the rich valleys, the flowing streams — but where is there a sentence written upon one of them that tells of salvation, of reconciliation to God, of access to a Father in Heaven?

I have heard exquisite echoes from the thunder rolling amidst Alpine heights, caught up and re-echoed from point to point. I have heard the dashing of the waterfall, the roar of the avalanche, the rushing of those torrents which form the vast rivers of Europe. I have heard the note of the nightingale, so touchingly pathetic on the summer night. But never from them all have I heard so sweet a note as this, "Come unto Me, all you that labor and are heavy laden, and I will give you rest." "Son, be of good cheer, your sins are forgiven!" "Enter into your closet, and when you have shut your door, pray to your Father who is in secret, and your Father who sees in secret Himself shall reward you openly."

Yes — here is our hope. Scripture revelation presents to man a door of access — it opens to the sinner a way by which he can draw near — it tells that even One, so just and holy, is accessible in the path which He has pointed out. This leads me to a third principle.

3. There can be no approach to the Father, except through the One Mediator. "I am the way, the truth, and the life. No man comes unto the Father but by Me." "You who once were far off, are made near by the blood of Christ." "Having therefore boldness to enter into the holiest by the blood of Jesus, by a new and living way, which He has consecrated for us through the veil, that is to say, His flesh. Having a high priest over the house of God; let us draw near with a true heart in full assurance of faith, having our hearts sprinkled from an evil conscience, and our bodies washed with pure water." (John 14.6; Ephesians 2:13; Hebrews 10.19-22.)

I direct the attention of the reader more especially to this last passage — it is one that can never fail to afford the Christian most precious help.

It tells plainly the ground of all confidence. The eye is fixed on the one great Sacrifice, the one all-sufficient Offering, the Blood of atonement, which removes every obstacle. It is not any laborious efforts, any strivings and strugglings, by which we have to force a way into God's presence. But the highway has been raised up, the door has been opened, there is no longer the least barrier or impediment to stay the course of the anxious seeking soul.

Sacrifices and offerings and burnt offerings, according to the law, the blood of bulls and goats, could never take away sin. But now Christ has been once offered to bear the sins of many. He has offered one sacrifice for sin forever. His one sacrifice is enough to remove the guilt of all mankind — it is so fragrant before God, that whatever person or gift or spiritual sacrifice it touches, that becomes also fragrant and precious before the most High.

Him for sinners bruised see,
Look through Jesus' wounds on me!

But we have more than this. We have not only the rent veil of our Savior's crucified body — but we have the living, interceding High Priest before the throne. When I fall low on my knees before. His footstool, I can point to the blood and its efficacy to give me a right of access.

That rich atoning blood,
Which sprinkled round I see,
Provides for those that come to God
An all-prevailing plea.

Still more: I can point to Him who pleads my cause before the mercy-seat.

I am unworthy — but He is worthy.
I am a frail child of dust — but He is the very Son of God.

I am at best but a sinner, in thought, in word, in deed — but He is the Holy One, the true Aaron, ever wearing the mitre, "Holiness unto the Lord." In His pleading, in His constant intercession, in His abiding advocacy in the presence of God — I have an unfailing ground of hope.

I learn, too, that I have a joyful liberty in my approach to God. I am invited to come with boldness! I am invited to draw near with a full assurance of faith. And the image employed sets this before me still more clearly. I may come unto the Holiest of all.

There was the court of the Gentiles; then next, the court of Israel; then next, the holy place, the court of the priests; and then, lastly, we come to the sacred enclosure of the Holy of Holies, where only the high priest, and he but once a year, was permitted to enter.

And now I learn here how very near I am permitted to come to God. Past the first court, past the second court, past the court of the priests — I may go as a priest, under the shadow of my great High Priest, within the veil — into the Holy of Holies, right up to the throne of the Most High — crying, Abba, Father!

Oh, what a privilege is this boldness of access! We are invited — yes, exhorted — to the enjoyment of it. The atmosphere of gloom and uncertainty, is not the atmosphere of true fellowship with God.

The region of asceticism, of legal fears, is not the land where God would have His people dwell. We must worship God with reverence and godly fear, for He is holy. But we must also come to Him with confidence, with joy, with freedom — unlocking to Him each secret chamber of the heart, unfolding to Him our secrets of sin and sorrow and care, for He is our most loving Father in Christ Jesus.

I can but remind the reader here how great a barrier to this confidence is raised up by the perilous and enslaving doctrine of Priestly Confession.

God has cast down the high wall of separation between Himself and His sinful creatures by the precious blood-shedding of His dear Son, and calls them on the strength of it to come straight to Him in fullest confidence.

Man immediately builds up a new wall, by stopping men on their way to God's mercy-seat — calling them aside to confess their sins to a human priest. If it be needful in any case that I should go to the footstool of a fellow-sinner, and receive through him Christ's absolution, then farewell all boldness! farewell all joyful access to God's presence! There is a barrier as high as Heaven between me and my God.

May God keep Christian people from this dangerous pitfall! May He manifest to them all that grace and mercy which may lead them close to Himself through His well-beloved!

There is yet one other foundation principle.

4. All true communion with God is the upspringing in the soul of the life imparted by the Divine Spirit. We have the Advocate with the Father pleading for us above — we have the Advocate in the heart, the Comforter pleading within. True communion is the fellowship of the Spirit — it is the Holy Spirit making intercession for us. The Savior speaks to the woman of Sychar of the only worship acceptable to the Father: "God is a Spirit — and they that worship Him must worship Him in Spirit and in truth." But whence can such worship arise? How possibly, in our carnal, earthly hearts, can anything arise so heavenly, so spiritual? May we not find the solution in the promise which the Savior had just before given to the woman: "Whoever drinks of the water that I snail give Him shall

never thirst; but the water that I shall give him shall be in him a well of water springing up into everlasting life."

What is all spiritual worship — but the gushing forth, the springing up of this living water?

Whence comes the first drawing, the first fervent desire for God?

Whence comes all true knowledge of Him whom we approach?

Whence comes the grace that overcomes the reluctance of our dead, cold hearts, to spiritual duties?

Whence comes it that we have an eye to discern the path into the holiest?

Whence comes all contrition, humility, perseverance, filial confidence in prayer?

Whence comes all this — but from the Spirit, the Author and Giver of life?

We have not received the spirit of bondage again to fear; but we have received the spirit of adoption, whereby we cry Abba, Father.

Here is a practical matter that much concerns the spirit of devotion in the Christian. Never forget your dependence upon the mighty aid of the Holy Spirit. Without Him you cannot think a right thought or offer a single acceptable prayer.

This spirit of Communion with God in the power of the Spirit is all-essential to our salvation. It is quite possible for people to live and die as members of Christian Churches, and yet never to possess it, and so to pass into the great future altogether unprepared. You may be a communicant, you may be a Sunday-school teacher, or a district visitor, or a collector for societies, or even one engaged in some way in God's house — yet, after all, the great question is, how far you are abiding in close fellowship with God.

The most sorrowful feature of the present day, in my judgment, is the low tone of spirituality in professing Christian people.

Too often family prayer is either neglected, or hurried over as a mere form.

Sunday morning is an excuse for late rising.

The souls of the children are little thought of.

Levity, and excessive dress, and show, and glitter, are plain and Levity, and excessive dress, and show, and glitter, are plain and unmistakable proof how much power the world retains over them.

Books of fiction are the ordinary reading, while . . .
God's Word is neglected,
and the prayer chamber deserted,
and the name of Jesus forgotten,
and holiness never cultivated,
and God put as far away, as if the fool's creed, "No God," were universally accepted.

And all this not in those who know nothing of religion, but who would think themselves greatly slandered if anyone imagined they were not Christians indeed.

Yet let the truth be spoken. If God be true, if the Word is sure and steadfast — such religion as this is a delusion and a sham! It is bad coin, and will ring false and hollow on God's counter. Yes, and it will bring a tenfold condemnation.

To have the light — and walk in darkness;
to know God's will — and not to do it;
to say, Lord, Lord — and yet not to strive after holiness;
to draw near to God with the lip — while the heart is far from Him
— what is this but to deceive yourself and to dishonor the Master, and at last to gain the sad rebuke, "I never knew you. Away from me, you evildoers!" Matthew 7:23

Dear reader, above all things cultivate reality and depth in your religion. If at last you would not prove a barren fig tree — keep up secret fellowship with God. Whatever you leave undone — never, never lose sight of the fact that secret communion with God is the most necessary part of your whole life. Let there be real, true, honest confession of sin. Let there be fervent, earnest petitions for the grace and help of the Holy Spirit. Let there be a few minutes given each day to a thoughtful meditation upon His Word. Ever hold it fast as assuredly true, that fellowship with the Father and the Son is the most sanctifying, the most strengthening, the most comforting thing in all the world; and that no man is a Christian in the sight of God who knows not the joy of a life of prayer.

Before I leave the subject, let me give a few HINTS to assist those who desire to keep near to God.

Take in the full consolation of the Fatherliness of God. Twelve times does Christ remind us in Matthew 6 of God being a Father to those who call upon Him. As a Father He is . . .

ready to forgive,
ready to hear,
ready to help,
ready to bless.

As a Father He pities and chastens and bears us in His arms. Yes, He is infinitely more than a father can be to his children. When reminding us that a father will give bread and fish, and all good and necessary things, to His children — our Lord adds, "How much more will your Father in Heaven give good things to those who ask Him." Our God is so good, so faithful, so true, so bountiful, so different from poor, fallen man — this, together with the thought that He is our Father in Christ, may lead us to lean confidently on His care, and trust wholly to His merciful provision.

The sympathy of Christ for us under all possible circumstances is a great help to a life of fellowship. We must believe that Christ has a sympathy towards every believer, and there is no position in which we can be placed in which we may not look for Him to undertake for us.

I have read of a bridge in Austria, and in twelve niches upon it there are figures of Christ under various representations. He is the King, the Priest, the Prophet, the Physician, the Shepherd, the Sower, the Pilot, the Carpenter, etc. And we are told that as men pass by they kneel by one of these figures. The countryman will kneel by Christ the Shepherd, the mechanic by Christ the Carpenter, the sailor by Christ the Pilot, the sick man by Christ the Physician, and so on. Each one selects the Christ that suits his own special need.

There is a blessed truth here. Whatever superstition may mingle with the thoughts of these men about the Savior, at least we may learn that no man can come to Christ without finding a special place in His heart for himself. We may learn that Christ has a grace to meet every condition in life — every sin, every sorrow, every temptation.

To bear this in mind is a link that binds us closer to our God.

We must have a wide area of prayer. We should take every circumstance that occurs, pleasant or painful, as giving us an errand to the throne of grace. In everything by prayer and supplication with thanksgiving, we must make known our requests unto God.

And we must cultivate a large spirit of intercession. It may begin with the necessities of our homes and families. It pleads for our congregations and parishes; for our schools and universities; for our villages, our towns, our cities; for our rulers and our ministers; for our brethren afar off and their flocks, either in our colonies or in heathen lands; for our home heathen, and the heathen who have not yet heard the Savior's name.

Make use of all the help you can find in maintaining communion with God.

The services of God's house, the regular and believing participation in the Sacrament of the Lord's Supper, the careful observance of times for private devotion — all these are very needful and helpful if used in a spirit of faith. They are golden pitchers — empty, indeed, and profitless, if only used in a formal way; but very blessed when filled with living water — the grace of the Holy Spirit.

Equally helpful is the daily searching into, and pondering the oracles of Divine truth. To listen to the voice of a friend to whom we are speaking, suggests fresh matter for interesting converse. In the Word, our Father speaks to us, and hence gives us new thoughts and desires toward Him, and enables us with more freedom to pour out our hearts before Him. Especially do Christian people find help in studying the Psalms. They greatly kindle our longings for God's favor and grace. "As the deer pants after the water brooks, so longs my soul after You, O God. Whom have I in Heaven but You? There is none upon earth that I desire beside You. Keep me as the apple of Your eye, hide me under the shadow of Your wings."

Then we may find help in each portion of the Lord's Prayer, in His example, in His promises to disciples, and His parables bearing upon this subject.

So also may we be quickened and strengthened by the prayers given to us in Paul's Epistles. (See Romans 15.13; Ephesians 1:15-23; 3:14-21; Philippians 1:9-11; Colossians 1:9-12; 1 Thessalonians 3:12-13; 2 Thessalonians 2:16, 17.)

Nor would I omit, in close connection with the help given from Scripture, the exceeding profit we may gain from the remembrance of Christian hymns.

Perhaps no one has ever left a richer legacy to the Christian Church than the late Miss Elliott, in the two hymns which are so greatly valued: the one for the penitent, the seeker, the soul that feels oppressed by the weight of sin —

Just as I am: without one plea,
But that Your blood was shed for me,
And that You bid'st me come to Thee:
O Lamb of God, I come!

This hymn was greatly valued by the late Rev. MacIlvaine. He left it as his wish that no address should be made at his grave, but this hymn sung. "It is my hymn," he writes: "expressing so sweetly the essence of the Gospel. It contains my religion, my hope, my theology. It has been my ministry to preach just what it contains. In health — it expresses all my refuge. In death — I desire that I may know nothing else for support than what it contains. When I am gone, I wish to be remembered in association with this hymn. I have no other plea — I can come in no other way."

The other hymn is for the child of sorrow and disappointment, for the careworn and the suffering Christian:

My God, my Father, while I stray
Far from my home, in life's rough way,
O teach me from my heart to say,
May Thy will be done.

Such hymns as these are most precious helps to those who are seeking nearer communion with God.

Lastly, I would say, if we would maintain communion with God, we must watch over our own heart and spirit. There must be a weaned heart, a heart separated from sin, from earthliness, from covetousness, from self-will, and all low aims. "If we claim to have fellowship with him yet walk in the darkness, we lie and do not live by the truth." 1 John 1:6

We must have a heart to rest in the will of God. He is the Only-Wise, the Only-Mighty, the Only-Good.

Rest on this anchor and be still;
For peace around your course shall flow.
When only wishing here below
What pleases God.

On every side the child of God is guarded by the watchful care of a loving Father. He may be tried, harassed, nearly overwhelmed by the waves of this troublesome world — yet the Most High is ever beside him. A remarkable expression is made use of in Psalm 32.11: "Whoever puts his trust in the Lord, mercy embraces him on every side."

It is even so: on every side he is shielded by Omnipotence.

Over him Jehovah stretches His sheltering wing: "He shall cover you with His feathers, and under His wings shall you trust."

Around him likewise there is sure protection: "As the mountains are round about Jerusalem, so the Lord is round about His people from henceforth, even forever." "I, says the Lord, will be unto her a wall of fire round about, and will be the glory in the midst of her."

So also beneath him: "The eternal God is your refuge, and underneath are the everlasting arms."

These words are rich in heavenly consolation. Spoken by Moses before he left the flock whom he had so faithfully led through the wilderness, they are written in Holy Scripture, bequeathed as the heritage of the whole Church. Sound their depths — upon your knees strive to realize the fullness of blessing they contain. If I can the very least assist any reader in doing this, my earnest desire in writing these words will be fulfilled.

"The eternal God is your refuge." He is your castle, your fortress, your dwelling-place: for provision, for shelter, for clothing, for defense, for rest, for the warm affection of home — repair there in your need. "Lord, You have been our dwelling-place in all generations." "The name of the Lord is a strong tower — the righteous man runs into it, and is safe."

"Underneath are the everlasting arms." That we may fully grasp the meaning of this assurance, there is a parallel expression that deserves our attention. Very frequent mention is made of "the arm of the Lord." It usually denotes the putting forth of Divine power, the active energy of the Most High God in the accomplishment of His purpose — either in the destruction of His enemies, or the preservation of His people.

It was by "a mighty hand and stretched-out arm" that He broke in sunder the bonds of the Israelites in Egypt. It was by the same glorious arm that He overthrew Pharaoh and his chariots in the Red Sea. It was thus, too, that He cast out the Canaanites, and gave Israel possession of the promised land; "for they got not the land in possession through their own sword, neither did their own arm save them; but Your right hand and Your arm, and the light of Your countenance, because You had a favor unto them."

It is of the triumphs of this arm, David sings: "You have a mighty arm, strong is Your hand, and high is Your right hand." And again: "His right hand and His Holy arm has gotten Him the victory."

It is this arm that has wrought our redemption. Isaiah prophecies thus: "The Lord has made bare His Holy arm in the eyes of all the nations; and all the ends of the earth shall see the salvation of our God." And thus the mother of our Lord rejoices in the anticipation of Him who shall be her Son, and yet her Savior: "He who is mighty has done to me great things, and Holy is His name. He has showed strength with His arm — He has scattered the proud in the imagination of their hearts."

Learn here, by contrast, the feebleness of the arm of man. "Have you an arm like God?" was the question put to Job. It is written again, "Put not your trust in princes, nor in the son of man, in whom there is no help." Without God, the arm of man is utterly strengthless, utterly powerless.

Very impressive is the way in which this truth is brought out in many of our readings. In a very marked manner do they set forth the inability of man to effect anything by his own unaided strength. "By reason of the frailty of our nature, we cannot always stand upright." "Almighty God, who sees that we have no power of ourselves to help ourselves." "Through the weakness of our mortal nature, we can do no good thing without You." "O God, without whom nothing is strong, nothing is holy." "The frailty of man without You cannot but fail." "Without You we are not able to please You."

Yet do not mistake here. Truly the arm of man of itself can effect nothing — but nerved and strengthened by the arm of God, it can effect marvels. Notice the words of Jacob in the blessing which he pronounced on Joseph, "His bow abode in strength, and the arms of his hands were made strong by the hands of the mighty God of Jacob." Was it not thus that Gideon overcame the Midianites? It was not the Lord without human instrumentality, but it was "the sword of the Lord and of Gideon." Was it not thus that David slew the giant? It was his own arm that slung the stone, and cut off the giant's head — yet it was in the name of the Lord Almighty that victory was given unto him. Therefore, Christian, neglect not to use your own arm, feeble though it be in itself. You cannot dispense with vigorous, active effort.

In the working out of your own salvation, labor and strive and fight. Resist sin to the very uttermost; aim at the highest mark; watch continually, that you be not led astray into error of doctrine, or laxity of practice. Yet ever remember where your strength lies — lean not on yourself, but on the power of Christ; He alone can make you more than conqueror.

From the very gates of Babylon, from amidst crafty and determined foes, through countless perils, and in a country full of rivers and mountains, did Xenophon lead safely the ten thousand Greeks home to their fatherland. Just so, from the very gates of the city of destruction, from amidst mighty foes, through mountains of difficulty —

does Jesus, the Captain of our salvation, by His own mighty arm, safely lead His chosen people to their everlasting home in the better country.

In the great conflict of these latter days, be courageous in fighting manfully on the Lord's side. Hold not back your arm. In the might of Jesus, you know not how much you may effect.

If you believe that Holy Scripture is indeed the very Word of God — if you believe that the pure Gospel, revealing a free and full salvation by reliance on the Crucified, is indeed the wisdom of God and the power of God — confess it boldly before men. Never think of taking neutral ground. If ever Christ required brave, fearless confessors, it is now.

Solon made it a law in Greece, that a man was dishonored and disfranchised who, in a civil sedition, stood aloof and took no part in quelling it. Another Lawgiver, wiser and greater than he, has said, "He who is not with Me, is against Me; and he who gathers not with Me, scatters abroad."

Yet here, again, while you are zealous on behalf of God's truth, rely only on the arm of the Mighty One. Jesus reigns supreme in Heaven and in earth. He sits above the waterfloods. He sits on the right hand of the Father until His enemies are made His footstool. All power is given to Him, who is the Head over all things for the defense of His Church. He can dispose the hearts of our rulers in Church and State to act wisely and boldly on God's behalf. He can pour forth His Spirit, and raise up standard-bearers for His truth. He can make His Word mighty as in the days of old. He can cast down error wherever it may be found — and build up in our day His Church, by fixing on the sure foundation many a living stone. For all this let us fervently, continually pray. "Awake, awake, put on strength, O arm of the Lord! Awake as in the ancient days, in the generations of old."

Oh, that Christians alone with God, in little groups of two or three, at the family altar, as well as in more public gatherings for prayer, would thus plead with God on behalf of our Zion. He would surely show Himself strong to save and help.

Read Acts 12. What could be more gloomy than the prospects of the Church as described in the commencement of that chapter? The King, a persecutor of the Church, one apostle slain, another in prison and threatened with the same fate. But though in fear of their lives, the little flock meet for prayer — and what follows? The whole aspect of affairs is changed. Peter is set free; the proud persecutor is brought low (he is eaten by worms,) "but the Word of God grew and multiplied."

And is not the arm of the Lord still as mighty as ever? "Behold, the Lord's hand is not shortened that it cannot save; neither His ear heavy that it cannot hear."

But turn now to the passage in Deuteronomy 33. The power of the Lord is here set forth as sustaining, supporting, upholding His Church and people.

"Underneath are the everlasting arms." It is not now the "arm outstretched" — but the "arms beneath," to keep and protect. And is there not a thought underlying these words that may render them still more precious than otherwise they would be? What is the figure employed here, but the little infant safely upborne in the arms of a nursing mother?

They are best explained by the words of Moses himself, as he complained to God that the burden laid upon him was almost more than he could bear. (Numbers 11.12.) "Have I conceived all this people? Have I begotten them that You should say unto me: Carry them in your bosom, as a nursing-mother bears the slicking child, into the land that You swore unto their fathers?"

Even so does Jehovah. carry His people through this earthly wilderness. "Listen to me, O house of Jacob, all you who remain of the house of Israel, you whom I have upheld since you were conceived, and have carried since your birth!" Isaiah 46:3

Or we may take the words as having a reference to the mother carrying her babe in her bosom. They apply in this case with equal force; and we know that this too is a figure which Jehovah has condescended to employ. "Can a woman forget her nursing child that she should not have compassion on the son of her womb? Yes, they may forget, yet will I not forget you."

In whichever way you take it, what a view does it present of the wondrous tenderness of the Divine compassion. Stay here and ponder for a moment the love of God toward His own redeemed people. It is the very joy of all joy, the very sweetness of all consolation, the very sun of our firmament, a river of endless pleasure — yes, our Heaven on earth and our Heaven above — to know assuredly that our Father loves and cares for us!

And it is in this parental character — this fatherly-motherly character of God (if we may use the expression) — that we most clearly discern how great His love is. "Behold, what manner of love the Father has bestowed upon us, that we should be called the sons of God."

Behold the depth of misery, need, and danger from which He has raised us! We read of Pharaoh's daughter finding the infant Moses, and making the child her own. What was her motive? Pure compassion. She saw the infant weeping; she knew he was the child of an enslaved race, and doomed to death. So out of mere compassion, she saved his life, provided for his necessities, brought him up in all the wisdom of the Egyptians, and purposed that he should have all the honor that would appertain to him as her son. Even so our Father beheld us in our lost condition, out of tender pity saved our souls from death, put us into His own family, and has provided all things to fit us for our position as the heirs of His kingdom.

Yes, far more do we discern His love, when we remember the means by which He has adopted us. He spared not His own Son from humiliation, from shame, from suffering, from death — that we rebels, outcasts, enemies, being made one with Christ, might rise to all the glorious privileges of his dear children. Oh, that the Holy Spirit, the revealer of all truth, might remove every veil from our minds, and display to us, in all its fullness, the love of our Father in Heaven!

Within the everlasting arms, is there a welcome for every returning penitent. Ever bear in mind the ready welcome which greets the sinner when he turns his foot homeward. The history of the younger son in the parable of Luke 15 places this beyond all doubt. It was a saying of

Augustine, "Are you afraid of God? Then run into His arms!"

What an illustration of this saying is found in the parable I refer to. The son was naturally afraid of his father's displeasure. The best he could expect was to be permitted to work as a hired servant. Yet he came back, trembling though it was. But what a meeting! "When he was yet a great way off, his father saw him, and had compassion, and ran and fell on his neck, and kissed him." Matthew Henry remarks here that the father had . . .

eyes of mercy — for he saw him;
affections of mercy — for he had compassion on him;
feet of mercy — for he ran;
lips of mercy — for he kissed him;
arms of mercy — for he embraced him.

Think likewise of the open arms of your compassionate Redeemer. He receives sinners, the very weakest and the very worst. When on earth, He cried to those about Him, "Come unto Me all you who labor and are heavy laden, and I will give you rest." He embraced in His arms the little children that were brought to Him. He refused none who sought His mercy and His aid. And at last, upon the cross, His arms were spread wide, as He endured all its agony and woe. Thus do we learn how earnestly He longs that the lost and perishing should flee to Him!

Reader, think of this. Past years have come and gone, and your life is yet spared. You have still the door of hope, the sure promises and invitations of the Gospel offered for your acceptance. If never yet you have known the Savior's love, if never yet in faith and prayer you have betaken yourself to Him as your High Priest, your Advocate — is it not time so to do?

What do you know of the changes that may come to you? What do you know, but this — that you cannot ensure the continuance of one single earthly gift, that long before another year or another month has run its course, you may be side by side with your fathers in the grave!

Is it not wise to be on the safe side? To know that, come what will, you have . . .
a portion you can never lose,
a hope that will never disappoint,
a rock under your feet that will never shake,
everlasting arms that will never let you fall?

Very earnestly would I plead with any in failing health, that without a moment's delay they would turn to the Sure Refuge. As I have noticed the feeble step, the wasted form, the distressing cough — the evident marks that the best part of life is over — I have often longed to commend to such the Savior who so tenderly feels for them. Should these pages be read by any who are thus suffering, may I beseech you, in Christ's name, no longer to shut your eyes to your own condition — no longer to buoy yourself up with the idea that you will before long recover — but to go in faith to Him in whom you shall have a life that will never end.

Wait not, tarry not — lest soon you should have no strength left for thought or prayer. The last attack may come very suddenly; and if you are not saved then — where are you? Why not now, even this very moment, lift up your eye to Jesus? While you read this, why not speak to Him thus: "O Savior, look upon my affliction, and forgive all my sin! Give me life through Your death. Visit not upon me misspent years, but even now receive me. Cleanse me in Your precious blood. Breathe Your Spirit upon my cold, dark heart. Draw me close to Yourself, and make me Yours forever. Amen."

These everlasting arms uphold forever every true believer!

The ark is floating on the waters of the deluge. It is borne hither and thiher by the violence of the waves; yet it never sinks, for these everlasting arms are beneath. At length it rests on mount Ararat, and Noah and his family go forth upon dry land.

A little boat is upon the lake of Galilee. A storm comes down upon the lake; danger appears to be imminent; the disciples cry out, "Master, master, we are perishing!" Yet were the terrified disciples reproved for their unbelief. That frail bark could never sink, for the everlasting arms are beneath.

That ark, that boat, represent the Church of Christ, upheld forever by Divine power and faithfulness. Amidst the surging tide of doubt, false doctrine, irreligion, and open infidelity — we might be ready to fear for its safety. But we can discern One Presence in the storm, and He is Almighty. He says, "It is I! Do not be afraid." And as Christ is near for the support of the whole Church, so likewise for that of each believing soul.

Christian reader, we would bid you take courage! We would bid you look forward with cheerful hope, as you journey heavenward. Have not the everlasting arms upheld you in days that are past? Has not the Lord brought you through many a sorrow, and many a sore temptation? Why then fear for the future? Can everlasting arms ever grow feeble, ever grow weary, through the lapse of years? Is not Jesus "the same yesterday, and today, and for ever"? Have you not the assurance, "The mountains shall depart, and the hills be removed — but my kindness shall not depart from you, neither shall the covenant of my peace be removed, says the Lord, who has mercy on you!" "I will never leave you, nor forsake you!"

True it is you may have to pass through great depths — yet these arms shall be lower still, they shall still be underneath you.

As Jonah sank beneath the wave, it seemed that he would rise no more — but these arms were there, and at length brought him safe to land.

David could cry, "Deep calls unto deep at the noise of Your waterfalls — all Your waves and billows are gone over me!" Yet he felt these arms were there; for he adds, "Hope in God; for I shall yet praise Him who is the health of my countenance, and my God!"

Jeremiah too could exclaim, "Waters flowed over my head; then I said, I am cut off." But not so, for the arms were there. He adds, "You drew near in the day that I called upon You. You said, Fear not."

Nor shall it be otherwise with you, than with these servants of God in old time — if only you trust in the name of the Lord.

You need not hide from yourself the probability, that some time or other during life's voyage you may have deeper trials than perhaps hitherto you have known. There may be deep, distressing anxiety about your temporal concerns — it need not be the fear of actual want, but that of being unable to meet your liabilities, and this may bring you many an unhappy day, and many a restless night. There may be pain — real, agonizing pain — that at times may almost terrify your spirit, that you know not how to endure it any longer.

There may be times of spiritual darkness and doubt; buffetings of the Tempter; hard thoughts of God that will force themselves upon you; evils that you abhor, and yet that cluster like bees around you. There may be heart-rending sorrows through the loss of life's companions; when the spirit, now for the moment utterly desolate, longs above all things for one more sight of the dear one that the Lord has taken.

There may be a depth of misery in connection with your home that may be utterly beyond all words to express.

It may be through some terrible disease which has touched one of its members.

It may be through the unfeeling conduct of a near relative.

It may be the wilfulness and waywardness of a child.

It may be that one whose soul is the burden of many prayers, determinately perseveres in a course of open ungodliness.

And perhaps, in addition to this, the great sorrow of your life, some other trial may be added, which seems to be the last feather of the burden that is ready to crush you to the earth.

Yet amidst any one or more of these depths, amidst all sinkings of heart — if you lean on Jesus, you may be sure the everlasting arms are beneath.

Be sure there is no woe altogether inconsolable, no sorrow altogether hopeless — since there is a Savior, a strong Redeemer, who knows how to comfort those that are cast down, and can open out a way of escape that you could never have imagined.

To any tried believer I would commend a few words out of the 10th Psalm. Mark the expression: "That You may take the matter into Your hand; the poor commits himself unto You — for You are the helper of the friendless."

There is quiet rest here — a light arises in the deepest darkness, when in all our conscious helplessness we commit both ourselves, and that which weighs sorely upon the spirit, into the hand of Him who is mighty to help and save. And is it not a matter of experience, that God does mercifully sustain the heart of His people, when otherwise they must utterly sink? They can feel, though they scarcely know how to describe — the gracious support afforded by the everlasting arms which uphold them.

The man who knows not Christ as His Savior, may indeed fall deeper and deeper, and find no strength, no peace. He may fall . . .
from one degree of sin to another;
from sins against the law — to sins against the Gospel;

from sins of ignorance — to sins against light and knowledge;

from lesser neglects — to a casting off all the restraints of religion;

from lighter offences — to daring rebellion against God.

He may fall into sorrows, where he is uncheered by a single ray of hope. He may fall, like Saul and Judas, into a state of terrible remorse. He may fall into soul-destroying errors, no less ruinous than open ungodliness. He may fall at length into that gulf of dark despair, that deep abyss of unfathomable woe, that wrath to come, which is the everlasting inheritance of Christless sinners! But with yourself, kept and guarded by the power of Him you love — oh how different shall it ever be!

The infant, nestling within its mother's arms, feels the warmth of those arms and of that bosom on which it lies. So shall you, reposing on Christ, sheltered in the bosom of Divine love, experience a heavenly peace, a holy joy, a calm rest and satisfaction, that surpasses knowledge. The very Comforter Himself shall dwell within you, enabling you to rejoice even in tribulation, strengthening your faith to hold fast the sure promises of the Word; yes, to lean confidently upon the care and the faithfulness of the Divine Promiser.

We have an illustration of the supporting grace of God, and the comfort of the everlasting arms, in the spirit manifested by the Rev. H. Budd, a native pastor of the Northwest American Mission. He writes home of the losses which he had experienced. His once large and thriving family is made quite a wreck. Within about six weeks he buries his son (who was also his fellow-helper in the ministry), his wife, and a loving and affectionate daughter nearly seventeen. Now, how does he speak of these heartrending afflictions?

"I do not for one moment doubt my Father's love. In all that has, in all that ever shall, befall me or mine — I own a Father's hand and a Father's love. My fond affection for those who have gone before me, would gladly have retained them in the world, that they might be a comfort to me in my declining years — but God has taken them out of my hands, to bring them into His own presence. I give way in thankful, adoring, weeping silence; and say: Even so, Father; for so it seemed good in Your sight!"

And be assured, though all the powers of earth and Hell were to combine, they should never wrest you from the embrace of the everlasting arms.

You may remember a touching incident with respect to Luther, in the wilderness of Wartburg. It is said that a rabbit, pursued by the hunter's dogs, crouched at his feet. He took it up, and hid it in his sleeve — but it was all in vain. The fierce dogs came up; and, scenting it in its hiding-place, violently tore it away from him. Then he thought of One stronger than he — His arm none could resist, and those in safeguard with Him no power should be able to pluck thence.

Oh, Christian, lie calmly, trustfully, securely, in the arms of your God. Fear not the reproach of man; fear not the storm that may rage about you — it shall only do His bidding, who in one moment can say, "Peace! Be still." Fear nothing but unbelief and sin. Fear only to grieve or wound the heart upon which you lie. Remember it is that of the Holy One — Him who is of purer eyes than to behold iniquity. Oh, dishonor not His holy name by the very least willful sin, by careless living, by a lukewarm spirit, or by any questionable compliances with the evil maxims or habits of a world that hates Him.

It was a warning, left by a very eminent minister of Christ, to such as had assembled around his death-bed: "Beware of such a religion as takes the doctrines of grace, without holiness in the daily walk! All such religion is a delusion!"

It is a true witness; therefore, take heed so to abide in the love of God, so to live by the faith of His dear Son — that every grace of the Spirit may dwell and grow in you — that your light may so shine before men, that they may see your good works, and glorify your Father which is in Heaven.

And if you yourself are upheld by the everlasting arms of your covenant God — ought you not to strive by all means to uphold your weaker brethren? "Bear one another's burdens, and so fulfill the law of Christ." "Lift up the hands which hang down, and the feeble knees." "Receive him that is weak in the faith."

Tenderly, hopefully regard any who appear to be arising to a new life, and to be seeking after God. Look not coldly upon them, but cherish the very first desire for good, and aid them by your sympathy and counsel.

Endeavor, if possible, to restore any who have fallen. A few gentle words may awaken the sleeping conscience. A letter kindly written may bring back the wanderer to the feet of Christ. Bear up in the arms of faith and prayer, the young of the flock — those that are yet weak in faith and knowledge, the needy, the suffering, the sorrowful.

Thus may you walk in the footsteps of Him who never broke the bruised reed, nor quenched the smoking flax — depending only upon His grace and strength.

"You will keep in perfect peace him whose mind is steadfast, because he trusts in you. Trust in the LORD forever, for the LORD, the LORD, is the Rock eternal." Isaiah 26:3-4

17154650R00105

Printed in Poland
by Amazon Fulfillment
Poland Sp. z o.o., Wrocław